inspiring stories for teens

25 lives that encourage you to overcome adversity, pluck up your courage and realize the self-confidence to achieve your dreams

By Dave Schafer

Acknowledgements:

Thank you to my own teenager, Quinn Schafer, for her advice and skillful copyediting of this manuscript.

Table of Contents

introduction

"Aroused, animated, or imbued with the spirit to do something." "Outstanding or brilliant in a way or to a degree suggestive of divine inspiration." "Mentally stimulated to do or feel something."

There are a lot of definitions of what being inspired means, but words can't really capture "inspired." It's a flicker of adrenaline-surging, fist-pumping, you-can't-stop-me attitude. It's a slow burn that sustains you when the world seems to be telling you that you're not good enough, or that you can't "do that." It's the moment when you see things differently, when you can do something in a new, better way.

That's what this book is about: Using words to give you that feeling of being inspired when maybe you're not feeling like doing much. In a world that feels divided, cynical and hopeless, we need an inspired new generation to insist on making things better. Hopefully, some of these stories strike a chord with you and inspire you to create your mark in the world as you become an independent adult.

Here are 25 stories of real people overcoming a variety of real adversities. Poverty, discrimination, disabilities, bullies, rejection and so much more—stories of those who have come before you. These people initially had few resources, yet they left enduring marks on the world. They're proof that it doesn't matter where you come from or where you are today, you can accomplish great things if you work hard and stay determined.

In the end, you determine the life you live. Here are 25 examples of that.

Each profile kicks off with a quote. The quotes aren't from the profiled person or even about them. They're general quotes to reinforce the more profound point that the profiled life teaches us. Each profile ends with a box that has two parts: "WHAT'S INSPIRING ABOUT [THE PERSON'S] STORY?" and "WHAT CAN YOU TAKE FROM THE STORY?" The former succinctly recaps the featured story, but without a lot of the details. The answer to the latter question encourages you to internalize what you can learn from the story. That way, you benefit from what you just read.

You can pick and choose which stories in this book speak to you and just read those, or you can start at the beginning and read all the way through. I think they're all fascinating stories, so I think you'll enjoy them. I've attempted to tell you their complete stories, but I encourage you to check out these people online for further information. For example, you can see what they look like with a simple Google search. I've cited my sources of information at the back of the book so you can have confidence that I'm not making this up and you know where to start if you want more information.

However you read through *inspiring stories for teens*, be sure to read the conclusion. That's the story of "The Forest Man of India," and it talks about planting seeds for a better future. That's what I hope you do after reading these stories: Plant your own seeds to build a better future for yourself and, if that's what you desire, the wider world.

Enjoy and be inspired.

chapter 1: overcoming established social roles

In a world where societal roles and expectations often confine people to narrow paths, the four women profiled here defied the status quo—and changed the world for the better by doing so. The actions they took are commonplace today: running a marathon, being a physician, holding public office, composing music for public performance. But when these remarkable women did them, they were blazing the trail that others now frequent.

Their stories inspire us to try new things, examine the roles society has established for us and determine if those roles are based on logic and facts or just used for oppression or "because it's always been that way." If it's because of oppression or tradition, then it's our duty to tear down those roles to open new avenues for ourselves and others.

These women dared to follow their dreams even when society told them they could never make those dreams reality. Well, they did.

And so can you.

Elizabeth Blackwell

first female Doctor of Medicine in the United States

"I am no longer accepting the things I cannot change.
I am changing the things I cannot accept."
ANGELA DAVIS

Twenty-nine medical schools rejected Elizabeth Blackwell's application for admittance. Still, she kept sending out applications, and the 30th school she applied to accepted her—as a joke.

It wasn't a joke to Blackwell, though, and she took advantage of the opportunity to change American society and the medical community.

Blackwell was born in February 1821, well before women were welcomed in medical practices. Her prosperous, cultured family lived in Bristol, England, until moving to the United States in 1832, first to New York, then to Jersey City, New Jersey, and finally to Cincinnati, Ohio. Blackwell's father died soon after arriving in Ohio, leaving the family poor. In response, Blackwell and her two older sisters opened a private school.

Blackwell enjoyed teaching but didn't find it engaging. In her diary, she wrote that she felt "the want of a more engrossing pursuit." She discovered that pursuit when her friend Mary Donaldson was diagnosed with cancer and told Blackwell that the ordeal was made worse by being attended to by a male physician.

"She told me, 'If I could have been treated by a lady doctor, my worst sufferings would have been spared me,'" Blackwell wrote. Donaldson suggested Blackwell become a doctor, an idea that grew on Blackwell.

"For weeks, I tried to put the idea suggested by my friend away, but it constantly recurred to me," she recalled.

Blackwell told friends that she was thinking of applying to medical school, but they scoffed at her. Medicine was no place for a woman; it involved human nudity, deadly diseases and gruesome scenes.

Better for Blackwell to remain a teacher.

Most physicians at the time were trained through apprenticeships with experienced doctors. This was primarily for men; the few women who apprenticed could only hope to become unlicensed physicians. There weren't many medical schools, and none accepted women.

One group of supporters did approve of Blackwell's desire to enter medicine, however: her family, which was progressive enough to be involved in movements to abolish slavery and secure the right for women to vote. But they warned her that she would likely face more rejection if she continued to pursue this goal.

In 1846, she began applying to medical schools. As the rejections poured in, Blackwell became more determined. "The idea of winning a doctor's degree gradually assumed the aspect of a great moral struggle, and the moral fight possessed an immense attraction to me," she wrote. Even while getting letters of rejection, Blackwell continued studying medical textbooks and taught herself Greek.

Blackwell wrote to prominent doctors asking for their help getting her into medical school. Only one wrote back: Joseph Warrington, a well-respected physician in Philadelphia. He responded that he was impressed with her ambitions but doubted any medical school in the United States would accept her. He advised her to become a nurse instead.

In response, Blackwell redoubled her efforts. She moved to Philadelphia in 1847 and met with Warrington, who was impressed with Blackwell's earnestness and determination. The two quickly became friends. He let her use his medical library, attend his lectures and accompany him on house calls. Warrington even wrote her a letter of recommendation when she applied to more schools.

Blackwell, while awaiting responses from her latest round of applications, continued to introduce herself to local physicians in Philadelphia, including one who outright laughed at her when she told him she wanted to be a physician. Another doctor, though, offered to give her anatomy lessons.

Finally, in October 1847, she got an acceptance letter from the dean of Geneva Medical School in upstate New York. Warrington's letter had convinced him to put up Blackwell's application for consideration by the student body; the students—all male—thought it was a joke and voted unanimously to admit Blackwell.

Blackwell had finally gotten into medical school. Now came the next challenge.

At Geneva, Blackwell's classmates and professors discriminated against and ostracized her. Professors made her sit apart during lectures, often omitted her from labs and barred her from demonstrations. Residents shunned her as a "bad" woman for rebelling against her gender role.

Still, Blackwell persevered. She ranked first in her class when she graduated in 1849, becoming the first female Doctor of Medicine in the United States.

Blackwell's training wasn't yet complete. She traveled to England and Paris for further training. Doctors in Europe mainly regulated her to midwifery or nursing. In Paris, she contracted an eye infection that left her blind in her left eye, forcing her to abandon her quest to become a surgeon.

Unfortunately, challenges remained when she returned to the United States. Discrimination against women physicians meant that she had few patients and a difficult time finding clinics and hospitals where she could practice her craft.

After being rejected for a position in the women's department of a large city dispensary, she opened her own dispensary to treat poor women in 1853. A dispensary is like a clinic; it distributes medications and medical supplies and, in some cases, even provides medical and dental treatment. Blackwell's was a single room in which she saw patients three afternoons a week. The dispensary was incorporated as the New York Infirmary for Women and Children a year later, and her sister, Emily Blackwell, and another colleague joined the practice. It was the first dispensary in the United States staffed by and for women.

In 1868, Blackwell opened the Woman's Medical College of New York Infirmary with 15 students and nine teachers. The college provided training for female physicians and medical care for the poor. Elizabeth Blackwell was professor of hygiene and Emily was professor of obstetrics and diseases of women.

No longer would a female be denied medical training just because of their gender. By never accepting social roles or "her place" in society, Blackwell ensured that.

"It is not easy to be a pioneer—but oh, it is fascinating! I would not trade one moment, even the worst moment, for all the riches in the world," she said.

Blackwell would go on to great success in the medical field. She became a professor of gynecology at the new London School of Medicine for Women. In January 1859, she became the first woman to have her name placed on the British medical register. She also helped establish the National Health Society and published an autobiography, 1895's *Pioneer Work in Opening the Medical Profession to Woman*.

Blackwell retired from practicing medicine in the late 1870s but remained a promoter of reform and women in medicine until her death in 1910.

WHAT'S INSPIRING ABOUT ELIZABETH BLACKWELL'S STORY?

Elizabeth was mocked when she said she wanted to study medicine. "That's not a lady's role," she was told. "Women don't do that." But she never backed down in her quest to attend school and train as a physician. She found allies along the way and not only got into medical school but excelled in her studies. Eventually, she opened her own school for women who wanted to study medicine.

WHAT CAN YOU TAKE FROM THE STORY?

If nobody else is doing it, so what? If society and even your friends tell you that this isn't a role for you, so what? Believe in yourself, even when you're confronted with rejection. Don't let doubters discourage you from taking the steps necessary to accomplish your goals—and possibly great things!

Frances Perkins

U.S. Secretary of Labor

"You never change things by fighting the existing reality.
To change something, build a new model that makes the existing
model obsolete."
RICHARD BUCKMINSTER FULLER

When asked if her gender was holding her back, Frances Perkins, the first female member of a U.S. presidential cabinet, said, "Being a woman has only bothered me in climbing trees." In an era when women's career and lifestyle opportunities were limited, Perkins didn't let being a female hold her back any other way.

Journalists of her day condescendingly called Perkins "Frances the Perk" and "Ma Perkins" because of the plain, matronly clothing she wore. Perkins, who was secretary of labor from 1933 to 1945, dressed that way as a concession to the attitudes of the day; she knew that men would only—maybe—be comfortable with a woman in public service if that woman looked like their mother.

President Franklin D. Roosevelt appointed Perkins despite a frantic outcry of opposition from labor leaders and others who didn't want a female secretary of labor. Her appointment was a significant milestone, and she would end up having a profound impact on citizens' lives, an impact that we still feel today thanks to her pivotal role in shaping the New Deal and the establishment of the 40-hour workweek, workers' compensation, and a minimum wage.

Perkins was born Fannie Coralie Perkins in 1880 in Boston, Massachusetts, and grew up in a middle-class family. Her parents were strict, and Perkins and her sister, Ethel, were constrained mainly to the people and events within their home and the nearby Plymouth Congregational Church. Her passion for social welfare started early; when she realized there were poor kids at school, she asked her parents why nice people could be poor. They gave her the standard answer of the time: That poverty was caused by alcoholism or laziness and that a little girl like Perkins shouldn't concern herself with the problem. But she did.

It was unusual for women to attend college, but Perkins enrolled in Mount Holyoke College, majoring in physics and minoring in chemistry and biology. She enrolled in the most challenging classes and became class president her senior year. During her final semester, she took a course in American economic history that required her to observe working conditions in the mills along the Connecticut River. That was an eye-opening experience.

"From the time I was in college, I was horrified at the work that many women and children had to do in factories," she later said. "There were absolutely no effective laws that regulated the number of hours they were permitted to work. There were no provisions that guarded their health nor adequately looked after their compensation in case of injury. Those things seemed very wrong. I was young and was inspired with the idea of reforming, or at least doing what I could, to help change those abuses."

When Florence Kelley, executive secretary of the National Consumers League, spoke to Holyoke's chapter of that organization, Perkins saw the possibility—and necessity—of a career in social work. The National Consumers League is a private, nonprofit advocacy group that represents consumers on marketplace and workplace issues.

After Perkins graduated in 1902—and against her parents' wishes—she sought a job in social work but couldn't get hired. So, she turned to the same profession as so many other women of the time, with their limited options: She became a teacher. This was in Lake Forest, Illinois, and during her free time, she worked at the Chicago Commons and Hull House, two settlement homes. Middle-class volunteers would live in these settlement homes in poor urban areas, sharing their knowledge and culture with nearby low-income residents. The settlement houses provided daycare, English classes, healthcare and other services to improve the lives of the poor people in the area.

That experience hardened Perkins' determination to do social work: "I had to do something about unnecessary hazards to life, unnecessary poverty. It was sort of up to me. This feeling ... sprang out of a period of great philosophical confusion which overtakes all young people," she said.

In 1907, her career in public service started when she became general secretary of the Philadelphia Research and Protective Association, an organization designed to prevent newly arrived immigrant girls from being lured into prostitution by phony employment agencies. Then, in 1909, she took a fellowship with the New York School of Philanthropy, where she investigated childhood malnutrition among children in Hell's Kitchen.

Everything she saw simply reinforced to Perkins the need—and urgency—for her to step up and do something to improve society, particularly for the working poor and children.

Then, on March 25, 1911, Perkins witnessed the Triangle Shirtwaist Factory fire. She watched as 47 workers—primarily women—jumped from windows on the eighth and ninth floors to their deaths on the pavement below to escape burning to death. In all, 146 people died in less than one hour, most of them Jewish and Italian immigrants. The fire illustrated the cramped, imprisoned conditions factory workers were forced to endure to make a living.

That was the day the New Deal was born, Perkins later said.

She became the executive secretary of the Committee on Safety that was created in the wake of that fire to recommend practices to prevent similar tragedies. By this time, Perkins was executive secretary of the New York City Consumers League. This role focused on establishing sanitary regulations for bakeries, factory fire protections, and limits on how many hours women and children could work in a factory in a week.

In 1918, she was appointed to the New York State Industrial Commission and became the highest-paid woman in public office. When she was promoted to industrial commissioner, Perkins discovered that, in spite of widespread corruption, politics could effectively yield social welfare legislation. She joined Roosevelt's cabinet when he was New York governor in 1929 and went with him to the White House when he became president in 1932. At the meeting where he offered her the job of secretary of labor, she arrived with a "note of practical possibilities" that outlined what would become the New Deal.

The New Deal would become a Big Deal. During the Great Depression, this program greatly increased the role of the federal government in people's lives—for good or bad—and redefined its role in handling economic and social issues. It provided immediate economic relief and reformed the agriculture, finance, waterpower, labor and housing industries. Meanwhile, the passage of The National Labor Relations Act in 1935 protected worker rights and allowed them to join unions and engage in collective bargaining. That addressed some of the labor issues that concerned Perkins.

Perkins remained a forceful advocate for workers and public works programs for the entirety of Roosevelt's presidency. But she faced resentment from people in the labor movement, the media and Congress who felt that a woman shouldn't be in such an influential role, and they took every opportunity to tear her down. For example, in the early days of the Red Scare—a time of public fear and worry over the supposed rise of communist or socialist ideologies in the United States—Perkins was branded a communist and Congress tried unsuccessfully to impeach her.

Perkins died May 14, 1965, and has been largely forgotten. History books and modern discussions of the New Deal call it Roosevelt's program, and it was because he implemented it as president. But make no mistake: Much of the New Deal was born from and championed by Perkins. In 1944, Collier's magazine did a profile on Perkins, in which it called the New Deal "not so much the Roosevelt New Deal as ... the Perkins New Deal."

If Perkins had stuck to "her place" in society, though, society would be a much different place today. Instead, she set an example for other women—and, really, for everyone—that even in the face of scorn and opposition, we can accomplish great things if we remain focused and committed.

"The door might not be opened to a woman again for a long, long time, and I had a kind of duty to other women to walk in and sit down on the chair that was offered, and so establish the right of others long hence and far distant in geography to sit in the high seats," she said.

WHAT'S INSPIRING ABOUT FRANCES PERKINS' STORY?

Frances's family told her she should take a traditional teaching position and live at home until she met a suitable man for marriage. Instead, she forged her own path of advocacy and took on a role that, until then, was unheard of for a woman. By blazing a trail, she opened the door for other women to become influential public figures and made a significant impact on society.

WHAT CAN YOU TAKE FROM THE STORY?

Don't let previously defined roles limit what you think you can accomplish. When someone tells you that it's not your place to try to do something that you want—or need—to do, say, "So what?" and do it anyway. Maybe you'll change the world, too.

Fanny Mendelssohn

composer and pianist

"Constraints can spur creativity and incite action, as long as you have the confidence to embrace them."
TOM KELLEY

When famed composer Felix Mendelssohn performed for Queen Victoria at Buckingham Palace on July 9, 1842, the queen agreed to sing one of her favorite songs from his portfolio of compositions: "Schöner und schöner schmückt sich" (which translates to "Decorates more and more beautifully").

Felix later wrote to his mother of the incident: "Then I had to confess—I found it very hard, but pride goeth before a fall—that Fanny had written that song, and would she now sing one of mine?"

"Fanny" was Fanny Mendelsshon, his older sister by four years. While Felix was undeniably a brilliant composer, so was Fanny. At the time, however, women were discouraged from pursuing a career in music. So, Felix would soar to international fame—yes, even using some of Fanny's compositions—while Mendelssohn would toil in relative anonymity until after her death. But because she didn't simply accept society's standards, Fanny Mendelssohn would eventually get the recognition she deserved and pave the way for future generations of female composers and musicians.

Mendelssohn was born into a prosperous family in Hamburg, Germany, in 1805. Her musical talent was apparent from a young age, and her parents provided her with a thorough musical education from renowned teachers beginning at age 11. Her mother, who had been taught by the renowned Johann Sebastion Bach, taught Mendelssohn how to play the piano. Mendelssohn composed her first piece at 14.

In 1820, she and Felix joined the Sing-Akademie music society, directed by composer Carl Friedrich Zelter. Zelter was impressed by the young Fanny Mendelssohn, telling the author Johann Wolfgang von Goethe that "this child [Mendelssohn] really is something special."

Despite their educational support, Mendelssohn's parents didn't consider music a viable career for their daughter. Her father, Abraham, forbid her from publishing her compositions and is quoted as saying, "Music is likely to become a profession for Felix, while it is only an ornament for you; it may never form the core of your life."

Felix admired his sister's ability and valued her musical opinion; they worked closely together and often asked each other for feedback. But Felix supported her father's ban against publishing her music.

Fanny Mendelssohn, though, didn't let the prohibition stop her. She just had to be content with a smaller crowd while her brother played big concert halls and even Buckingham Palace. At 17, Mendelssohn, a superb pianist, began performing Sunday concerts at the family home, concerts that often included more than 100 guests. Those Sunday performances would be the primary stage for her music during her lifetime—she only performed publicly twice, once at age 12 when she played all 24 of the preludes from Bach's "Well-Tempered Clavier" and at a charity concert in 1838. At the charity concert, she performed Felix's "Piano Concerto No. 1."

While society discouraged Mendelssohn from performing and claiming her musical pieces publicly, her husband, Wilhelm Hensel, was supportive. He put a blank piece of paper on her music stand every morning as an enticement to write.

Although she couldn't make a career out of it, Mendelssohn never stopped writing: She composed more than 400 pieces, including about 120 pieces for piano, many art songs, and chamber music, cantatas and oratorios. Her compositions displayed a blend of lyricism, emotional depth, and technical complexity. Felix, as we've seen, gladly usurped some of her pieces; he published six of her songs under his name and performed other pieces without giving her credit. But we can't be too hard on the guy; there was no outlet for Fanny Mendelssohn to release her pieces, and at least Felix ensured they were heard.

In 1846, at age 40, Mendelssohn finally began publishing songs under her name, becoming one of the first women composers to do so. Unfortunately, Mendelssohn died from a stroke just a year later. Felix, who had a lifelong bond with his sister, was heartbroken by her death and died from a stroke six months later.

Mendelssohn's music was forgotten and overshadowed by her more famous brother's compositions for a long time. But that's changing;

historians are discovering that, besides her published works, some pieces authored by "F. Mendelssohn" and long attributed to Felix were written by Fanny. For example, "Easter Sonata," discovered in 1970, was proven to be composed by Fanny. In 2012, it was performed in Fanny's name for the first time.

It took more than a century and a half, but Mendelssohn is finally getting the respect and recognition she deserves, not only for her ability but also for her role as a trailblazer among female composers. And that's only possible because she never let "the rules" of society prevent her from doing what she loved and excelled at.

WHAT'S INSPIRING ABOUT FANNY MENDELSSOHN'S STORY?

In the 1800s, it was unladylike for a woman to perform music in public. So, even though Fanny demonstrated massive talent in playing piano and composing musical pieces, she was discouraged from publishing her works or performing publicly. Despite this, Fanny wrote more than 400 pieces—musical works of art that are appreciated to this day. Although there was no future in it, Fanny continued to write music. Years later, these works were published under her name and the perception of what a woman can do musically changed forever. In this way, she paved the path for future generations of women to become professional composers and musicians.

WHAT CAN YOU TAKE FROM THE STORY?

Even when established societal views tell you there's no reason to pursue your dreams and goals, that you can't profit off it or make a difference in the world, keep going. As is proven many times in this book, the people who tell you there's no reason to pursue your dreams are right—but only until you prove them wrong.

Roberta "Bobbi" Gibb

trailblazing runner

"How many times must you be told?
There's nowhere that we don't go."
L7

"Women are not physiologically capable of running a marathon," the letter told Roberta "Bobbi" Gibb in 1966. It was from the organizers of the Boston Marathon in response to Gibb's entry form to run in that year's marathon.

She had anticipated finding her competition number in the package. Instead, she got a slap in the face.

The letter explained that the Amateur Athletics Union prohibited women from running more than 1.5 miles; marathon organizers couldn't risk the liability of allowing Gibb to compete. Furthermore, women who participated in sports were considered "unattractive." Kathrine Switzer, who ran in the 1967 Boston Marathon, said, "The idea of running long distance was always considered very questionable for women because an arduous activity means you would get big legs, grow a mustache and your uterus was going to fall out."

In the 1928 Summer Olympics, women competed in track and field events, including the 1500-meter, 10,000-meter, and *the marathon*. Three of the nine women who ran the 800-meter final broke the world record. That's great, right? A demonstration that women could undoubtedly compete in running events. However, newspapers worldwide undermined the accomplishment by incorrectly painting the event as a disaster. The *Chicago Tribune* reported that five women collapsed after the race and that the fifth-place finisher had to be "worked over" after she fell unconscious on the grass at the end of the race. The article claimed that silver medalist Hitomi of Japan needed a 15-minute revival period because of exhaustion. *The New York Times* repeated the claims, as did international newspapers.

The papers used this exhaustion to show that running even 800 meters was too hard and "dangerous" for women. The *Montreal Daily Star* called the race a "disgrace" and suggested that the event be erased from future Olympics because "it is obviously beyond women's powers of endurance."

The fact that the race winner, Lina Radke of Germany, and five other finishers beat the previous world record (held by Radke) in the qualifying heats was barely mentioned and certainly not held up as a reason for the exhaustion.

The Congress of the International Amateur Athletic Federation promptly voted to eliminate the 800-meter run. It wasn't held in the Olympics again until 1960.

Although it was nearly 40 years after those 1928 Olympics, Gibb stepped into a similar environment in 1966. There were still fears that playing sports would make women more masculine and sap their baby-making strength.

Gibb never backed down. She'd always been energetic, and her mother once told her, "You're never going to find a husband while running around woods with the neighborhood dogs."

She lived close to the Boston Marathon route, and in 1964, her father took her to watch the event. "I just fell in love with it. I found it very moving," she later said. "All these people moved with such strength, courage, endurance and integrity. Something deep inside told me that I was going to run this race—this was what I was supposed to do."

And no committee of men stuck in inherited misogyny was going to stop her. She began training on trails and paths where disapproving eyes wouldn't see her; her boyfriend would drop her off on his motorbike and she'd run home. She drove her parents' VW campervan across the country for 40 days by herself, and when she stopped, she'd run for up to 40 miles a day.

Finally, she was ready. She applied for her runner's number. But the marathon organizers weren't ready for her.

"I realized that this was my chance to change the social consciousness about women," she said. "If I could prove this false belief about women wrong, I could throw into question all the other false beliefs that had been used to deny women opportunities.

"If I can show that a woman can run 26 miles, and run it well—stride for stride with the men—that is going to throw all the rest of the prejudices and all the misconceptions and all of the so-called reasons for keeping women down that have existed for the past how many centuries? Centuries of this stuff! And so, I sort of chuckled to myself and thought, 'Oh, this is going to be fun! I'm going to turn the whole thing on its head.'"

Gibb, 23, took a four-day Greyhound bus trip from her home in San Diego to her parents' home in Boston. When she arrived, she announced to her startled parents that she was going to be the first woman to run the Boston Marathon. She pulled on her brother's Bermuda shorts and an oversized sweatshirt over top of a swimsuit. When she arrived at the marathon, she pulled up the hood. At the starting area, she crept into some nearby bushes.

After the starting gun went off, Gibb waited to let the faster runners pass. Then she pumped her legs and unofficially joined the other runners.

"Very quickly, the men behind me could tell that I was a woman— probably by studying my anatomy from the rear," she said. "I was so nervous. I didn't know what would happen. I thought I might even be arrested."

But rather than opposition, she was met with support. Spectators yelled, "Way to go, girlie!"

"There was this myth that men were always against women, but it wasn't true. Those guys were great, upbeat, friendly and protective; they were like my brothers," Gibb said.

When Gibb told the other runners about her fear of being kicked out of the race, they assured her they wouldn't let anybody do that.

Soon, Gibb removed her sweatshirt and ran proudly with her blond ponytail swinging from side to side. As she neared Wellesley College, a women's university, pandemonium erupted.

"Word spread to all of us lining the route that a woman was running the course," said Diana Chapman Walsh, who was a senior at the college that day and was the college's president from 1993 to 2007. "We scanned face after face in breathless anticipation until just ahead of her, through the excited crowd, a ripple of recognition shot through the lines, and we cheered as we never had before. We let out a roar that day, sensing that this woman had done more than just break the gender barrier in a famous race."

Gibb said: "The women were crying and jumping up and down. One kept shouting 'Ave Maria, Ave Maria'. It was an emotional moment for me."

Three hours, 21 minutes and 40 seconds after starting to make history, Gibb crossed the finish line—ahead of two-thirds of the other runners.

Maybe women can run a distance, after all.

Gibb set out to prove a point. And she did. "It changed how people thought about women running," she said.

In 1972, women were finally issued number bibs for official entry in the marathon.

WHAT'S INSPIRING ABOUT BOBBI GIBB'S STORY?

In the 1960s, society still believed that women were too fragile to run long distances. Running in a marathon was dangerous, and so they weren't allowed entry. For Bobbi, this wasn't good enough. She knew she could run the 26.2 miles, and she set out to prove it. She accomplished her goal by surreptitiously joining the race—and then beating two-thirds of the men to the finish line. Six years later, the Boston Marathon began allowing women to join the annual event.

WHAT CAN YOU TAKE FROM THE STORY?

When you face unfair or illogical opposition, challenge it. Don't accept something that is "common knowledge" without testing it. And if you find it to be untrue, fight back against that assumption, even if it means sneaking into the arena.

chapter 2: overcoming failure and rejection

After a chapter profiling only women, we have a chapter that features only men. Men who faced down failure and rejection and kept plugging away to accomplish their goals. Men who think of failure as a necessary step to success and that rejection is just the result of people not understanding the next great thing.

Their stories serve as a testament to the power of resilience, determination and unwavering belief in oneself. Hopefully, you finish it with a belief that if you persevere, you will accomplish your goals, too.

Jack Ma

businessman, investor and philanthropist

"A rejection is nothing more than a necessary step in the pursuit of success."
BO BENNETT

Jack Ma scored a one on the math portion of the standardized university entrance test—out of a possible 120. When he retook the test, his score only improved to 19.

Not exactly the score you'd think would lead to future riches and an incredibly successful career in business. But Ma never let these scores, or his struggles with math in general, limit him.

Ma (whose name in Chinese is Ma Yun) was born on October 15, 1964, in Hangzhou, a city of 2.4 million people in the southeastern part of China. He grew up in a communist country isolated from the West, and his family didn't have much money. Despite his scrawny build—Ma even now stands at just 5 feet, 7 inches—he often got into fights with classmates. "I was never afraid of opponents who were bigger than I was," he wrote in *Alibaba: The*

Inside Story Behind Jack Ma and the Creation of the World's Biggest Online Marketplace.

He wasn't afraid of hard work, either. After then-U.S. President Richard Nixon visited Hangzhou in 1972, the town became a tourist magnet. At 12, Ma began waking up at 5 a.m. every morning and riding his bike 40 minutes to an international hotel. There, he offered his services as a guide to tourists in exchange for English lessons. He did that for nine years, no matter the weather conditions. Over that time, his English improved markedly.

Despite his drive and skills, his family's lack of money and connections prevented him from advancing in society without an education, so Ma applied for college. That's when he failed the math portion twice. Rather than give up and accept a life of lesser, Ma studied and passed the math exam on his third try. His score was enough to get him into what Ma called "Hangzhou's worst college," Hangzhou Teacher's Institute.

After graduating in 1988, Ma married his college sweetheart. He applied for more than a dozen jobs, including at a local KFC, a hotel and the police department, but was rejected every time. So, he taught college English for $12 a month for five years.

Ma continued seeking ways to get ahead—and finding failure. He opened an English training school with 20 students. Three years later, the school's enrollment was still 20 students, so he closed it.

In 1992, he opened the Hope Translation Agency. To support the venture, Ma went to nearby cities and bought goods that he would resell for a higher price. His work for this agency led Ma to the United States in 1995, when he first saw the Internet. Ma instantly understood how this new global community could change the world, and he wanted a part of it.

When he returned to China, Ma founded China Yellow Pages, which created websites for companies. He invested about 20,000 Chinese Yuan (about $2,800 in today's U.S. dollar) into the new venture; about 7,000 was his money, and more than 10,000 was from his sister's family. This was almost all the money Ma had. The company office was a single room with a workstation and an old PC.

One problem, though: It wasn't possible to access the Internet in his hometown at that time. Despite this fact, Ma preached the potential power of the Internet to his friends and convinced some of them to hire him to design websites for them. These friends described their business to him, and he wrote down the details in English and sent them to a company in Seattle. His friends in Seattle built the website and took screenshots of it for Ma to share with the client.

It's impressive that Ma convinced anyone to invest in a website in that situation, much less spend the equivalent of US$2,400 for a site, which is what Ma charged. "I was treated like a con man for three years," he later said.

This company, too, struggled, and Ma left it when the company was bought by Hangzhou Telecom two years after its founding.

But Ma wasn't discouraged: "If you don't give up, you still have a chance. Giving up is the greatest failure," he said.

Finally, in early 1999, during a meeting in his apartment, Ma and 17 others agreed to build Alibaba Group (Alibaba.com), a business-to-business (B2B) online marketplace. The site, which lets exporters post product listings that buyers could peruse, quickly attracted members from all over the world. By October 1999, the company had raised more than $25 million in capital. Ten years later, its market value was $5 billion.

Today, Alibaba, which has expanded to provide consumer-to-consumer (C2C), business-to-consumer (B2C) and B2B sales services, digital media and entertainment, logistics, and cloud computing services, is more profitable than competitors Amazon and e-Bay—combined.

Ma, meanwhile, has a net worth of more than $30 billion, according to Bloomberg. That's math that he can probably do, even though it once seemed impossible that he would ever be in such a position.

Because Ma never accepted rejection and learned from his failures, he made his dreams come true—likely beyond even his wildest imagination.

WHAT'S INSPIRING ABOUT JACK MA'S STORY?

Jack scored a one on the standardized math test—out of a possible 120—which prevented him from being accepted into university. So, he retook the test. And when he failed again, he studied harder and passed on his third try. Then, he was rejected for jobs dozens of times—but still, he kept applying. When he wanted more than a teaching career, he started a business—which failed. So did his next business and the one after that. But still, he continued to create enterprises until he found one that became successful. Not only did Jack never accept rejection, but he also learned from his failures and came back more prepared the next time.

WHAT CAN YOU TAKE FROM THE STORY?

Perseverance. Failure isn't the end of an endeavor. "Giving up is the greatest failure," Jack says. He also says, "If you've never tried, how will you ever know if there's any chance?" So, even when confronted with rejection and failure (and failure again), keep believing in yourself. One more quote from Jack Ma: "No matter what your current condition, how or where you grew up, or what education or training you feel you lack, you can be successful in your chosen endeavor. It is spirit, grit and hardiness that matter more than where you start."

Sir James Dyson

design engineer

"Fall seven times and stand up eight."
JAPANESE PROVERB

James Dyson created 5,126 failed designs of a vacuum cleaner over five years—but, boy, did the 5,127th design knock it out of the ballpark.

Dyson introduced the first dual-cyclone vacuum cleaner in 1993. Instead of a bag that collects the dirt and debris that the vacuum sucks up, this vacuum has a fast-spinning motor that creates a powerful centrifugal force to separate dust and debris from the airflow. This creates sustained suction and a deeper clean.

That invention turned Dyson into a British Knight Bachelor and a billionaire. But he was no overnight success.

Born in 1947 in Cromer, Norfolk, in the United Kingdom, Dyson suffered the loss of his father when he was just 9 years old. While studying architectural design at the Royal College of Art, he conceived the unique design of a mushroom-shaped theater for a well-known theater director. Dyson asked inventor and engineer Jeremy Fry for project funds, but Fry turned him down.

Fry did ask Dyson to design an adaptable, high-speed landing craft, and Dyson created the Sea Truck. Fry became a mentor and hired Dyson to lead his company's Marine Division.

While working there, Dyson had the idea for a nontraditional plastic wheelbarrow, one with a load-spreading, pneumatic ball made from molded plastic rather than a wheel. Its wide-leg design prevented it from sinking into soft ground. He called it the Ballbarrow.

In 1974, Dyson resigned from Fry's company to focus on creating the Ballbarrow full-time. He released the first version that year. Four years later, while spraying the Ballbarrow's metal frame with powered paint, Dyson became frustrated by the wasted excess powder that missed the frame. That paint got caught in the cloth behind the Ballbarrow and became clogged. Dyson decided to find a better way.

He got the idea for a cyclone vacuum after noticing an industrial cyclone used to get rid of wood dust in a sawmill. So naturally, he built a 25-foot cyclone to suck away excess powder when working with his Ballbarrow.

Around this same time, he was also frustrated that the non-reusable bags in the top-of-the-range Hoover vacuum cleaner his family had bought frequently clogged. He decided to see if the same technology could work in the vacuum cleaner as in the sawmill. However, designing the cleaning tool was no easy feat; he had to miniaturize the motor to fit inside the vacuum cleaner while keeping it strong enough to create the necessary centrifugal force.

His first attempt to do so failed. So did his second. And his 100th. And his 1,000[th]. As mentioned previously, so did his 5,126[th].

"Everyone gets knocked back. No one rises smoothly to the top without hindrance. The ones who succeed are those who say, 'Right, let's give it another go,'" he has said.

Dyson gave it another go, and design 5,127 worked.

His new vacuum, though, was rejected by British retailers, who didn't see the practicality of Dyson's innovation. Of course, that didn't stop him. Japanese retailers were more receptive, and the first Dyson vacuum cleaners were only sold in that country.

Finally, in 1993, he launched his first mass-produced vacuum cleaner, the DC01. Now British retailers, and sellers around the world, saw the benefits of the bagless cleaner, and Dyson's vacuum manufacturing company grew.

Not everything Dyson subsequently created worked out. The Contrarotator washing machine, which used two contra-rotating drums to mimic the actions of hand washing, was deemed too expensive to produce. He designed a battery-electric vehicle that could travel more than 600 miles on a single charge and measured a little more than 16 feet in length, providing room for seven adults. Unfortunately, it was deemed commercially nonviable, and production was halted before it ever rolled off the assembly line.

On the other hand, Dyson also created the Airblade hand dryer, which uses focused blasts of air to dry hands in 10 seconds. And, as he continues to learn from his "failures," there are surely more to come—all because he doesn't see failure as an endpoint but rather as the next starting point.

"I made 5,127 prototypes of my vacuum before I got it right. There were 5,126 failures. But I learned from each one. That's how I came up with a solution. So, I don't mind failure," he has said.

WHAT'S INSPIRING ABOUT SIR JAMES DYSON'S STORY?

Trying something you've failed at a second or even a third time takes courage. How about if you fail at it more than 5,000 times? Who would continue trying when giving up in frustration would be so much easier?

James Dyson, that's who. With a tenacity that infuses all his attempts at innovation, James kept at it until he figured out how to get the bagless cyclone vacuum design to work. And in doing so, he changed household cleaning.

WHAT CAN YOU TAKE FROM THE STORY?

Understand that failure isn't the end; it's a lesson to help you achieve great things. So don't give up. When you get frustrated, take some time away. But return to what you're trying to accomplish, incorporate the lesson from your last "failure," and keep at it. You may be surprised how often this proves to be the formula for success.

James said: "Successes teach you nothing. Failures teach you everything. Making mistakes is the most important thing you can do."

Colonel Harland Sanders

businessman and founder of Kentucky Fried Chicken

"Today's rejection may become tomorrow's acceptance."
EHSAN SEHGAL

At age 45, Harland David Sanders was serving fried chicken at his restaurant in Kentucky—a restaurant so popular that the state's governor designated him an honorary Kentucky colonel. That chicken would eventually make Sanders wealthy and internationally recognized, but he had to go down some rough roads to get there, roads beset with poverty, failures, setbacks and rejections.

Sanders was born on September 9, 1890, in Henryville, Indiana. His father, a farmer and butcher, died when Sanders was 5, and his mother would be away from the family for days at a time working in a tomato cannery plant. Sanders cared for his two younger siblings. This was when he started cooking, becoming especially skilled at baking bread and cooking vegetables and meat.

He dropped out of school in the seventh grade and worked as a farmhand, horse carriage painter, streetcar conductor and other jobs from ages 10 to 16. While he worked hard, he wasn't getting ahead and was moving from job to job without advancing in a career; at that point, it didn't look like he had an exceptionally bright future.

At 16, Sanders enlisted in the United States Army by falsifying his age on the form. He was honorably discharged a year later, forcing him to return to labor, this time with a railway company.

Next, Sanders worked as a steam engine stoker for three years until he was fired for "insubordination" after he got ill. He went back to railroad work but lost that job after getting into a fight with a colleague. While working there, though, he met Josephine King, whom he married in 1908. Sanders' struggles to hold a steady job put stress on their relationship. After he lost his railroad job, Josephine took their three children and moved back in with her parents in another state.

Also while working at that railroad, Sanders pursued a law degree through a correspondence course. He received his lessons and assignments in the mail and mailed back his completed assignments. He then practiced law in Little Rock, Arkansas, for three years and earned enough money for his family to move back in with him.

But his career as an attorney ended after he got into a courtroom brawl with his client.

His next job was a life insurance salesman, but he was dismissed by that company for insubordination. In his mid-20s, he moved back in with his mother and returned to work in the railroad industry.

He was more successful with the ferry boat company he established, which operated on the Ohio River. He eventually sold that for the equivalent of $393,000 in today's money and used that as seed money for a new company that manufactured acetylene lamps. That venture failed, however, after a competitor started selling its electric lamps on credit, making it more accessible for buyers.

It wasn't looking good for ol' Harlan Sanders. But, although it didn't seem that way at first, his fortunes began to turn after he lost his job running a Standard Oil service station in Nicholasville, Kentucky. The station closed because of the Great Depression. The Shell Oil Company offered to let Sanders use one of its stations in North Corbin, Kentucky, for a restaurant rent-free—he just had to pay the company a percentage of his sales. This is where Kentucky Fried Chicken was born. Sanders served chicken, steak and country ham dishes out of his restaurant and earned that "Colonel" designation.

But Sanders' heartache wasn't over yet. In 1932, the couple's second child, Harland Jr., died because of complications from a tonsillectomy.

Then, in 1939, a fire burned the restaurant to the ground. Sanders rebuilt it as a 140-seat restaurant and motel, but gas rationing during World War II—which meant fewer tourists on the road or needing overnight stays—resulted in the closure of that location, leaving him with just a little savings and $105 from Social Security.

But by then, he'd finalized his "secret recipe" that included frying the chicken in a pressure fryer, which cooked it faster than traditional pan frying. After the war, he decided to turn his recipe into a franchise and traveled the country trying to sell businessmen on the idea of a restaurant serving his locally famous chicken.

But: There were no takers.

Sanders endured 1,009 rejections before a chain restaurant owner and operator in Utah, Pete Harman, agreed to franchise his recipe in 1952 and open the first Kentucky Fried Chicken restaurant. The sign painter, Don Anderson, coined the name.

Harman's new restaurant had tremendous success, and other restaurant owners soon franchised the recipe. The agreement called for them to pay Sanders $0.04 from every sale his recipe generated.

Franchising took off, and Sanders had finally "made it." By the time Sanders sold the company for $2 million in 1964, there were more than 600 KFC franchises in the United States, Canada, the United Kingdom, Mexico and Australia. (Today, there are more than 25,000 KFC restaurants in more than 145 countries and territories worldwide, according to KFC's website.)

When Sanders died at 90, he was worth about $3.5 million. Likely only Sanders could have imagined such a thing when he was struggling so badly that his family had to leave him and move in with his in-laws, or when he was dismissed for "insubordination," or when he lost his reputation as a lawyer after fighting with his client.

WHAT'S INSPIRING ABOUT COLONEL HARLAND SANDERS' STORY?

The Colonel faced many hardships and setbacks, but he never let those obstacles and failures stop him. Harland continued to reach for the next thing, the next job or innovation that would provide him and his family with the life he wanted. Even when he was touring the country and receiving more than 1,000 rejections for his "golden idea" of a chicken recipe, he kept going.

"One has to remember that every failure can be a steppingstone to something better," he has said.

WHAT CAN YOU TAKE FROM THE STORY?

Never give up, no matter how badly things seem to be going for you. If you keep striving, you can accomplish your goals and dreams. If you have a dream, take the first step, and don't quit until you've made that dream a reality.

"I think a dream is just a suggestion to start something out, do something," Harland said.

chapter 3: overcoming anxiety

In a National Health Interview survey of teenagers, 21% of respondents reported experiencing symptoms of anxiety in the past two weeks. The National Institute of Mental Health estimates that 49.5% of adolescents have had a mental health disorder.

So, if you feel irritable, tense or restless, or you have trouble concentrating because of a sense of impending doom, danger or panic, you're not alone. If you feel that you're not worthy—of your accomplishments, of your gifts, of living—you're certainly not the only one. Even household names—successful people whose lives seem filled with wealth and adoration—feel that way.

Anxiety has no "lane." It attacks people of all races, socioeconomic situations and genders.

But, as you'll learn from the profiles in this chapter, if you can reject that demeaning voice telling you you're not worthy and that the world is too big or too dangerous for you, you can accomplish great things. It's not easy, and you're going to need help. There's no shame in that. But with help, you can overcome the anxiety that seeks to limit you and live a life of fulfillment and impact. Just ask Kevin Love and Tessa Zimmerman.

Tessa Zimmerman

Founder and Executive Director at Upstream Education

"You don't have to control your thoughts.
You just have to stop letting them control you."
DAN MILLMAN

When Tessa Zimmerman was 13 years old, a therapist told her that she'd never go to college and would live at her parents' home for her entire life. That's how bad her anxiety disorders were.

"I'm proud to say that the therapist was absolutely wrong," Zimmerman wrote after finishing college, moving out to live on her own, and starting a nonprofit organization.

As a young girl, Zimmerman suffered severe anxiety and panic attacks. She tells the story of her third-grade teacher assigning the classroom a simple writing prompt: "What did you do this weekend?" Zimmerman couldn't do it. She remembered what she had done, but putting it down on the page was impossible. She'd write a word and then erase it. When her teacher couldn't help her, Zimmerman burst into tears and suffered her first panic attack.

The teacher sent Zimmerman to the principal's office.

That cycle continued for years; Zimmerman would have a panic attack and teachers wouldn't know what to do about it. They thought it was a behavior problem. "I spent the vast majority of my elementary and middle school years in the principal's or guidance counselor's office," she wrote.

Zimmerman started believing that she was a bad child, and she writes that she became afraid of herself. By seventh grade, she was having several panic attacks a day.

Now, Zimmerman understands what was happening. When she reacted to stimuli, she often chose anxiety. She went into fight-or-flight mode, a response that served our ancestors well when they encountered saber-tooth tigers or other predators and needed to determine whether to run or stand and fight. In extreme, physically demanding environments, this automatic response can mean the difference between life and death. When dealing with a writing prompt, not so much.

Perhaps Zimmerman's life would have continued on this path, and she indeed would have never attended college, if a family friend hadn't recommended Easton Country Day School to her parents. It's a private school that prioritizes the whole child, meaning it focuses on holistic well-being and optimizing conditions for social and emotional well-being. This approach recognizes how important a child's social, physical and emotional health are to their learning.

The school's principal, Mr. Quirk, believed in preparing students for the "inevitable stressors and anxieties of life." He taught them about mindfulness and positive psychology. "Mental health was not a conversation reserved for a health class once a week; rather, every morning, Mr. Quirk would lead my high school through a mindful body scan to help us start our days," Zimmerman wrote.

His teachings helped Zimmerman get a grip on her anxiety and panic attacks and learn to *respond* to stimuli rather than react with that fight-or-flight mentality. Now, she could pause, go inward and respond from a place that "feels good" rather than from fear.

"I'll be honest; I do not magically wake up and feel like this. I have to rely on daily tools to keep choosing joy and stop myself from reacting with anxiety," she wrote in her book, *I Am Tessa*.

No longer chained down by her anxiety, Zimmerman proved that therapist wrong. She graduated Summa Cum Laude with a degree in entrepreneurship from the Watson Institute. In 2024, Forbes named her to its "30 Under 30" list of educators. "The truth is we all have a choice in how our story unfolds, anxiety disorder or not," she wrote.

Now, Zimmerman is helping others craft the life they want. She founded Upstream Education to keep Mr. Quirk's impact and presence alive and to equip more educators with the tools he instilled in her. The nonprofit has affected more than 60,000 students by making mental health just as important as academic success.

To learn more about Zimmerman and her methods for coping with anxiety and panic attacks, check out *I Am Tessa*.

To learn more about Upstream Education, visit www.upstreamedu.org.

WHAT'S INSPIRING ABOUT TESSA ZIMMERMAN'S STORY?

When Tessa was told to accept a life constrained by her anxiety and panic attacks, she refused. She and her family found an educator who understood what was happening to her and how to help her deal with her anxiety. This allowed her to succeed in school—and as the founder and executive director of a nonprofit that is now assisting other educators to understand the importance of the "whole student" approach to teaching and the methods that can be used to deal with anxiety and panic attacks.

WHAT CAN YOU TAKE FROM THE STORY?

Check out Tessa's book for details on how she fights off her panic attacks. If you're dealing with anxiety, understand that you're not alone—a *lot* of teens are dealing with that. If you're being punished or misunderstood because of this, don't give up. Seek out a professional to help you control your responses and don't stop until you find the solution that works for you.

Kevin Love

professional basketball player

"Don't believe everything you think!"
ROBERT FULGHUM

Kevin Love left an NBA game in 2018 "with an illness," according to media reports. But the truth is he left because he had a full-fledged panic attack while playing for the Cleveland Cavaliers.

"I thought I was dying. It was just an out-of-body crazy experience that I'd never had before," he later wrote.

Although he had not experienced the out-of-body feeling before, he was familiar with the anxiety that caused it. Love, the son of a former NBA player, was a top-ranked prospect when he graduated from Lake Oswego High School in Oregon.

"I think for me growing up in Portland, Oregon, it was the anxiety to perform, to fit in, also the pressure I put on myself, the pressure really from coaches, parents, maybe even the community, that was very high . . . I think everybody expected a lot from me, a lot from my teams, a lot from my coaches," he later said.

After a season of college basketball at the University of California, Los Angeles, where he led the team to a Final Four appearance in the 2008 NCAA Tournament, he was taken fifth overall in the NBA draft. He had great success in his NBA career: he was a five-time All-Star, two-time member of the All-NBA team, World Champion with the Cavs in 2016, and gold medal winner with the U.S. national team at the 2010 FIBA World Championship and 2012 Summer Olympics.

But for much of that time—and since childhood—Love dealt with anxiety and depression. They would manifest in different ways, and he would deal with them as a child by "going somewhere and having a rage-type fit." He described the experience of anxiety as a "never-ending feeling in the pit of my stomach," continuing: "I had this sense that I was doing something wrong. I never was. I just had that feeling for no reason."

He was racked by impostor syndrome, not feeling worthy of everything he'd achieved. He'd look in the mirror and tell himself he's not good enough.

He used these periods of depression as competitive fuel. In that way, it may appear as though this was a good thing. But his identity became wrapped around his on-court performance, and that brought him to dark places.

"You can't achieve yourself out of depression. You can't achieve yourself out of that high level of anxiety," he has said.

As many of us do, he sucked it up and went about his day. It seemed unmanly to ask for help. "It was a form of weakness that could derail my success in sports or make me seem weird or different," he said.

But it got worse, he writes in *The Players' Tribute*:

> It got to the point that year where I was simply paralyzed with depression. And of course, I'm not about to show my weakness to anybody, right? I was tucked away in my apartment, and nobody could see me suffering. The only time I would leave my apartment was to work out, because that was the only place where I felt like I added value to the world, period. To those around me, I would put on a brave face.

> Fake facades are hard to keep up.

> The future started to feel meaningless. And when it gets to the point where you lose hope, that's when the only thing you can think about is, "How can I make this pain go away?"

After that 2018 game in Cleveland, he knew something had to change. He came into the game stressed about family issues, and the Cavs were struggling early in the season. He hadn't been sleeping well. The expectations were weighing on him.

He writes in *The Players' Tribute* that he knew something was off right after tipoff. He was winded within the first few possessions, and his game was "off." He made just one basket and two free throws in the 15 minutes he played in the first half. Then, when he arrived at the bench during a third-quarter timeout, his heart was racing faster than usual. He had trouble catching his breath, and everything was spinning. It was "like my brain was trying to climb out of my head."

When the huddle broke up, he couldn't physically reenter the game. Cavs head coach Tyron Lue sensed there was something wrong. Love said he'd be right back and then ran to the locker room. "I was running from room to room like I was looking for something I couldn't find. Really, I was just hoping my heart would stop racing. It was like my body was trying to say to me, 'You're about to die.' I ended up on the floor in the training room, lying on my back, trying to get enough air to breathe."

That was the end of the game for him—and the beginning of confronting his anxiety and depression.

Someone accompanied Love to the Cleveland Clinic for tests, all of which came back as normal. He was relieved but concerned about what had happened. Two days later, he scored 32 points in a game. He was glad to be back on the court and feeling more like himself, but he was bothered that, more than that, he was more relieved that very few people knew about why he'd really left that game. Why was he so concerned about people finding out the truth?

> It was a wake-up call, that moment. I'd thought the hardest part was over after I had the panic attack. It was the opposite. Now I was left wondering why it happened—and why I didn't want to talk about it. Call it a stigma or call it fear or insecurity—you can call it a number of things—but what I was worried about wasn't just my own inner struggles but how difficult it was to talk about them. I didn't want

people to perceive me as somehow less reliable as a teammate, and it all went back to the playbook I'd learned growing up.

This was new territory for me, and it was pretty confusing. But I was certain about one thing: I couldn't bury what had happened and try to move forward. As much as part of me wanted to, I couldn't allow myself to dismiss the panic attack and everything underneath it. I didn't want to have to deal with everything sometime in the future, when it might be worse. I knew that much.

The Cavs helped him find a therapist—even though Love had, until that moment, thought he was the last person who would have sought therapy. Despite his initial skepticism, the treatment helped. The therapist helped him develop coping mechanisms, and Love found level footing—while admitting that it can still be a struggle at times. And he says that it got worse before it got better.

Love would go on to write a widely hailed article in *The Players' Tribune* about his anxiety and depression, sparking a broader conversation among and about athletes. Talking about it, too, has helped him.

"It was something that before I pressed send on my first article with *The Players' Tribune*, I was really, I guess, scared would be the right word and uneasy and had a lot of anxiety, but, you know, it was, it just came a point in time and the perfect storm for me in that year that I just didn't want to live in the shadows anymore," he told the *Harvard Business Review*.

To help others come out of the shadows and deal with their anxiety and depression, Love has established the Kevin Love Fund, a charity that provides education, research and grants to help others with their mental health.

WHAT'S INSPIRING ABOUT KEVIN LOVE'S STORY?

Kevin "had it all"—wealth, championships, fame, a dream job in the NBA ... and anxiety and depression that he hid well. Until he couldn't. Then, he did the "unmanly" thing of seeking help and speaking out about his issues. He knew it wouldn't be a smooth path, but he was determined to take care of his mental health. And he has, although it continues to be a struggle. He also established a charity that provides education, research and grants to help others with their mental health.

WHAT CAN YOU TAKE FROM THE STORY?

That feeling of anxiety or worthlessness you have? You're not alone. Even the rich and famous feel that way sometimes. But there are resources out there for everybody, including you. It starts by talking to someone you trust about how you're feeling.

chapter 4: overcoming discrimination

Even in the 21st century, discrimination continues to be prevalent in society, affecting countless people. Some people continue to see others as "lesser" or feel threatened by people different than themselves.

But different doesn't mean "lesser." The profiles in this chapter are just three examples of that. There are countless inspiring stories of people who have risen above racial discrimination, demonstrating remarkable resilience and courage. The three lives recounted here not only overcame the barriers and prejudices imposed upon them but also became advocates for change, inspiring others to embrace diversity and stand against discrimination.

Their experiences serve as powerful reminders of the strength of the human spirit and the potential for positive transformation even in the face of adversity.

Alice Coachman

first black woman to win an Olympic gold medal

"We must open the doors and we must see to it they remain open so that others can pass through."
ROSEMARY BROWN

In 1939, Alice Coachman, a 16-year-old freshman at Madison High School in Albany, Georgia, broke the high school and college high jump records in the Amateur Athlete Union (AAU) national championship's track and field competition—in bare feet.

In a life of impressive athletic accomplishments, this was perhaps the most impressive because of what she'd overcome to get to that point. Due to her black skin color in the segregated South, Coachman didn't have access to facilities and organized sporting events, and her family didn't have money for equipment. Nor did her father, Fred, support her athletic endeavors. According to the National Women's History Museum, Fred whipped Alice for pursuing her athletics; he wanted her to sit on the front porch and look "dainty" like a "proper woman." His mindset wasn't uncommon in the 1920s and '30s. Many people at the time considered it unladylike for females to compete in sports.

But Coachman, the fifth of 10 siblings, wasn't to be discouraged—by her father, social norms or segregation. She devised her own training regimen, which involved running barefoot in fields and on dirt roads and using rope and sticks to improve her high jump. She also played softball and baseball with boys when she wasn't picking cotton, supplying corn to the local mills, or picking plums and pecans to sell to supplement the family's income.

By the seventh grade, she was one of the best athletes in Albany—male or female. But she still didn't have equal access to training facilities and couldn't train with white children or use white-only facilities.

Fortunately, the boys' track coach at her high school, Harry E. Lash, recognized Coachman's talent and took her under his wing. His guidance matched her determined spirit, and soon Coachman was winning AAU championships in the high jump; not just that first one in bare feet, but for the next nine years in a row! She won every title from 1939 through 1948.

After that initial barefooted win, Tuskegee Institute in Alabama (now known as Tuskegee University) offered her an athletic scholarship. Her parents gave their blessing for her to enroll. The scholarship required her to work while studying and training, so she cleaned and maintained sports facilities and mended uniforms.

She entered Tuskegee Institute in 1943 and would win national track-and-field championships in the 50- and 100-meter dashes, the 4x100-meter relay, and the running high jump during her time there. She also led the Tuskegee basketball team to three consecutive conference championships as a guard.

It only made sense that Coachman would take on international competition in the Olympics next. However, the 1944 games were canceled because of World War II, and in early 1948, doctors discovered she had a tilted uterus. They recommended that she not compete. She felt like a kid again, with her father telling her to give up athletics.

And just like when she was young, Coachman didn't relent. She had surgery to insert a rod in her back before leaving for the Olympic Games in London.

"I didn't want to let my country down or my family and school," she reportedly said. "Everyone was pushing me, but they knew how stubborn and mean I was, so it was only so far they could push me."

She certainly didn't let anybody down. On a rainy afternoon at Wembley Stadium, Coachman cleared the five-foot, six 1/8-inch bar on her first attempt to set a new Olympic record and win the gold medal. This made her the first black woman to win an Olympic gold—and the only American woman to win a gold medal at those games.

The win made Coachman a celebrity. She was featured prominently on billboards alongside Jesse Owens, a black man who was a four-time gold medalist. Famous jazz musician Count Basie threw her a party, and President Harry Truman congratulated her. A 175-mile motorcade that stretched from Atlanta to Albany welcomed her home, and an "Alice Coachman Day" celebrated her accomplishment in Georgia.

But discrimination mired the celebration of her accomplishment. In the Albany auditorium where she was honored, blacks and whites had to sit separately, and the white mayor refused to shake her hand. She had to leave the celebration by a side door.

Coachman's track career concluded after those games, at the young age of 24, leaving behind an astounding legacy of 34 national titles and an Olympic gold medal. Her journey of firsts continued in 1952, when she became the inaugural black female athlete spokesperson for Coca-Cola.

Coachman was inducted into nine halls of fame—including, of course, the National Track-and-Field Hall of Fame and the U.S. Olympic & Paralympic Hall of Fame. In 1994, she established the Alice Coachman Track and Field Foundation to support young athletes pursuing their dreams and help retired Olympic veterans. At the 1996 Olympic Games in Atlanta, she was honored as one of History's 100 Greatest Olympians.

Coachman's impact is not confined to her achievements. Her name lives on in the form of Alice Avenue and Coachman Elementary, a testament to her enduring legacy. Although she passed away on July 14, 2014, at the age of 90, her story continues to motivate and inspire generations.

"She opened doors that no one else could open," Tommie Smith told Team USA. Smith, a black man, won the 200-meter sprint finals and gold medal at the 1968 Olympics. "She literally started the liberation of women in sport. ... Had it not been for the Alice Coachmans of society, especially in our sport [of] track and field, I could have never been because I would have no portal to come through."

All because she never accepted it when others—her dad, society, her doctors—told her she shouldn't run and shouldn't challenge accepted roles and conditions. All because she didn't give up.

WHAT'S INSPIRING ABOUT ALICE COACHMAN'S STORY?

Alice never agreed with those who told her she wasn't allowed to accomplish her dreams. In the face of "You can't do that's"—from society, her family, and even her doctor—she continued to push herself and find ways to improve her running endurance and high jumping abilities.

"I've always believed that I could do whatever I set my mind to do," she said.

WHAT CAN YOU TAKE FROM THE STORY?

Just because others say you can't do something—maybe even that nobody has ever done that something before—doesn't mean you can't. You determine if you can do something through your hard work and dedication, nobody else.

George Washington Carver

American agricultural chemist

"Accomplishments have no color."
LEONTYNE PRICE

In 1885, George Washington Carver, who had been born into slavery but had been free nearly his entire life, was accepted into Highland College.

Accepted, that is, until administrators learned of his skin color. Then, the college withdrew the acceptance.

That was the way of things for Carver, who was penalized much of his early life because he was black. He persevered through it all to become a renowned educator and research scientist.

Carver was most likely born in 1864 in Diamond, Missouri. His father, Giles, died shortly after he was born, and about a week after his birth, marauders from Arkansas kidnapped Carver along with his sister and mother. All three were sold in Kentucky. The trio's owner, Moses Carver, sent a man to bring them back, but only baby George was found and returned to Missouri. He never saw his mother or sister again and was told that his mother and sister were dead, "although some say they saw them afterward going north with the soldiers," he wrote.

Carver nearly died from whooping cough when he returned to the Carver farm, and although he recovered, he would remain a sickly child. "My body was very feeble, and it was a constant warfare between life and death to see who would gain the mastery," he wrote. He also wrote that the family doctor told him he would never live to see 21 years.

That feebleness would play a prominent role in his future achievements because it kept him in an environment to learn rather than spending time doing manual farm labor. Sickly George often remained in the home doing domestic chores, such as cooking and embroidering.

After the emancipation of slaves, Moses and his wife, Susan, raised George and his older brother, James, as their children, giving them their surname. No local school accepted black students, so Susan homeschooled the boys, teaching them to read and write. This led Carver to develop a lifelong love of learning and search for knowledge, with music, painting, flowers, and sciences being his favorite subjects.

While living with his unofficial adopted parents, Carver often spent hours in the woods collecting flora, which he put in a little garden hidden in brush near the house. He kept it hidden because wasting time on flowers was considered foolishness. However, because vegetation thrived under his touch, those who knew him began calling him "The Plant Doctor."

Moses and Susan encouraged his learning, but their own knowledge was limited. So, at 11 or 12 (records are sketchy), Carver left this home to attend a school for black children. The school was in Neosho, about eight miles away; he never lived at the Carver farm again, although he did maintain communication with the Carvers and visit them often. In Neosho, Carver lived with a black couple, Mariah and Andrew Watkins, in exchange for helping with household tasks.

When Carver introduced himself, he did so as "Carver's George." Mariah told Carver that he should refer to himself as "George Carver."

There was another George Carver around, so our Carver later adopted the middle initial "W." The "W" didn't stand for anything except to distinguish him from the other George Carver. He signed letters as "George Carver" or "George W. Carver." However, once a reporter asked him if the "W" stood for "Washington." Carver supposedly replied, "Why not?" and the name stuck, even though it seems he didn't use it himself.

Carver attended several schools before receiving a diploma from Minneapolis High School in Minneapolis, Kansas. After the rejection by Highland College, he drifted across the country and settled in as a head cook at a large hotel in Winterset, Iowa. That's where he met a "Mr. & Mrs. Dr. Milholland," who insisted he go to Simpson College for art.

At the college, Carver developed his painting and drawing skills through sketches of botanical samples. Seeing his talent for drawing the natural world, a teacher suggested that Carver enroll in the botany program at the Iowa State Agricultural College (now Iowa State University).

Carver was the first black student at Iowa State. But he didn't let that isolation stop him; he earned undergraduate and master's degrees from the college.

After graduation, he set out on a career of teaching and research, including running Tuskegee Institute's agricultural department, starting in 1896. (Years later, you'll remember, Alice Coachman attended Tuskegee.) Tuskegee's agricultural department achieved national renown under his leadership with its groundbreaking research on plant biology, which led to the development of new uses for crops. This was particularly important because cotton production in the South was in decline at the time; overproduction had left the fields exhausted and barren. Carver suggested planting peanuts, soybeans and sweet potatoes instead to restore nitrogen to the soil.

Carver became a prominent expert in science and one of the most famous people of his time. Presidents Theodore Roosevelt, Calvin Coolidge and Franklin D. Roosevelt sought his advice on agricultural matters. Henry Ford and Mahatma Gandhi also sought his counsel on agriculture-related issues. He promoted science through his syndicated newspaper column and tours across the nation, during which he spoke about the importance of agricultural innovation. From 1923 to 1933, he spoke about racial harmony at white Southern colleges on behalf of the Commission on Interracial Cooperation—during a time when segregation was still the law of the land.

In his life, Carver invented hundreds of products, including more than 300 involving peanuts. (But not peanut butter!) In 1941, Time magazine dubbed him the "Black Leonardo." That same year, the George Washington Carver Museum opened on the Tuskegee Institute campus. The museum displays his scientific specimens and some of his paintings and drawings.

In 1943, the George Washington Carver National Monument was established on 240 acres that had been the Moses Carver farm. The monument, the first United States national monument dedicated to a black person and the first time in United States history that a birthplace site was designated as a national monument to someone other than a United States president, includes a statue of Carver and a nature trail, museum and cemetery.

Before that was established, though, Carver died on January 5, 1943, after falling down a flight of stairs. He left behind a legacy that was only possible because he never gave up on his love of learning and was fortunate to have people in his life who encouraged and helped further it.

"From oppressive and crippling surroundings, George Washington Carver lifted his searching, creative mind to the ordinary peanut and found therein extraordinary possibilities for goods and products unthinkable by minds of the past and left for succeeding generations an inspiring example of how an individual could rise above the paralyzing conditions of circumstance," Martin Luther King, Jr. said.

WHAT'S INSPIRING ABOUT GEORGE WASHINGTON CARVER'S STORY?

George had a thirst for knowledge, and he didn't let obstacles prevent him from learning. He took advantage of the opportunities he was presented with and sought out others. When wasting time on flowers was frowned on, he carried out his botany experiments in a hidden garden. When he was denied access to a whites-only local school, he traveled to a different town, living with strangers, so that he could attend school. Then he used his knowledge to innovate how we grow and use crops, particularly peanuts.

WHAT CAN YOU TAKE FROM THE STORY?

No matter your current circumstances, you can always find ways to learn about the things that interest you. Look for opportunities to gain knowledge, and don't be afraid to ask those who might be able to impart their information.

Ida B. Wells

journalist, suffragist and civil rights activist

"Where you see wrong or inequality or injustice, speak out, because this is your country. This is your democracy. Make it. Protect it. Pass it on."
THURGOOD MARSHALL

On May 27, 1892, the offices of the *Memphis* (Tennessee) *Free Speech and Headlight* newspaper, partly owned by Ida B. Wells, were burned to the ground by a white mob that, spurred on by white newspaper editors in the South, also threatened to hurt Wells and her family physically.

At the time, Wells, the first female co-owner and editor of a black newspaper in the United States, was out of town after publishing a series of articles and editorials in which she documented the atrocity of lynchings and argued that black men often weren't guilty of the "crime" for which they were lynched. Many of these "crimes" centered on the claim that the black man had raped a white woman. But she found that many of the lynchings actually occurred for minor offices or even noncriminal transgressions. These included not paying debts, being drunk in public, challenging white economic dominance or having consensual interracial sex.

"Nobody in this section of the country believes the old threadbare lie that Negro men rape white women," she wrote.

The idea that a white woman could find a black man attractive was too much for white men to handle. White newspapers began denouncing the editorials, calling her a "black scoundrel" and encouraging whites to avenge their women.

Wells never returned to live in Memphis or anywhere else in the South. But the intimidation didn't stop her. In fact, she would go on to become a staunch anti-lynching crusader and proponent of women's suffrage.

Wells was born in Holly Springs, Mississippi, on July 16, 1862. Her parents, James and Lizzie, were slaves, and even though the family would be freed when legal slavery ended, they still faced prejudices and discriminatory restrictions as to where they could go and who they could interact with.

James helped establish Shaw University (now Rust College) for newly freed slaves, and that's where Wells received her early schooling. Education was important for her parents; they insisted that their children get an education. However, when Wells was 16, both her parents and a sibling died in a yellow fever outbreak. Wells, as the oldest, suddenly became the head of the household, tasked with caring for her six remaining brothers and sisters. To support them, she took a job as a schoolteacher.

She wasn't going to let her new burden stand in the way of getting an education and building a prosperous life for herself, though. She continued going to school while cooking for the family and washing and ironing its clothes. She even found time to teach Sunday School.

Three years later, in 1882, Wells and her two youngest sisters moved about 50 miles northwest to Memphis to live with her aunt. There, she enrolled at Fisk University.

Of course, because she was still in the South, with its Jim Crow laws that enforced segregation, prejudice followed Wells. In 1884, she was forcibly removed from a train going from Memphis to Holly Springs. She'd ridden the ladies' car aboard the Chesapeake & Ohio Railroad train numerous times before with no problems. But this time, the conductor told her to move. When Wells refused, the conductor tried to drag her from her seat; Wells responded by biting him. That's when two men intervened to help remove her from the train.

Wells sued Chesapeake & Ohio Railroad and won a $500 settlement—which the Tennessee Supreme Court overturned. It was just another injustice Wells endured because of the amount of melanin in her skin.

During this time, Wells worked part-time as a journalist and publisher while teaching in a segregated school. But she was fired from the teaching job when she complained about the conditions of the school.

It was another attempt to silence Wells. It was another failure.

Instead, Wells turned her attention to journalism full-time, writing articles and editorials under the name "Iola." She was just 24. Three years later, she bought into the *Memphis Free Speech and Headlight,* becoming its editor.

She was in that role when her friend, Thomas Moss, and his two co-owners of a grocery store were lynched after hostilities with rival white grocers. Those grocers didn't like that Moss's grocery store was drawing business away from their stores.

Wells responded by writing editorials criticizing lynchings. She spent two months traveling across the South gathering information on lynchings.

The resulting articles and an editorial led to the mob burning down her newspaper offices. But, as noted, that didn't succeed in shutting her up, either.

Her friend, T. Thomas Fortune, a former slave, offered her a weekly column in his newspaper, the *New York Age*. Her first article for *Age*, which carried the byline of "Exiled," covered nearly the entire front page of the June 25, 1892, issue. It was a deeper, more graphic condemnation of racism, terror and violence inflicted on black people in the South than had previously been reported in newspapers. She also listed more than 700 instances of lynchings, with the dates, places and victims' names. To forestall claims that she was exaggerating or lying, she took all her information from white journalists and white-owned newspapers.

Of course, there was plenty of backlash at Wells after the article was published, but Wells remained steadfast. From then on, she helped frame public opinion against lynching. Years later, she added securing women's right to vote to her crusades. She was also a founding member of the National Association for the Advancement of Colored People (NAACP). The NAACP fights for civil rights and helped pass the 1957 Civil Rights Act, the 1960 Civil Rights Act, the 1964 Civil Rights Act, the 1965 Voting Rights Act, and the 1968 Fair Housing Act.

In 1895, Wells told a newspaper reporter that she still occasionally got death threats intended to get her to stop her work against lynching.

"Does it scare you any?" the reporter asked.

"I haven't quit yet," she replied.

WHAT'S INSPIRING ABOUT IDA B. WELLS' STORY?

Ida spoke up when she saw injustice, even in the face of censorship and violence—threatened and carried out. She knew that she was risking her life by writing about lynchings, but she was determined to change perceptions. And she did.

WHAT CAN YOU TAKE FROM THE STORY?

Don't let fear stop you from accomplishing great things. Follow your dreams, even when it becomes uncomfortable to do so or when others try to stop you. If they're trying to stop you, then they're getting uncomfortable, and you're doing something right.

chapter 5: overcoming skeptics

We all suffer from criticisms and naysayers. For a teenager, those doubts can take on a life of their own and become the narrative by which you live. But it's in these moments of doubt and skepticism that we have the opportunity for the greatest personal growth and transformation.

Any success will require you to ignore those doubters and forge ahead. That's what the two men profiled in this chapter did. They faced doubts about their abilities, criticisms of their ideas, and skepticism about their potential for success. Yet, they didn't let skepticism deter them. Instead, they used it as fuel to propel them forward. Their stories are a testament to the power of resilience, inspiring us to push past the doubts of others and achieve greatness.

When someone tells you you'll never amount to anything or you're not good enough, respond as you would when your parents tell you that you can't go to that midnight party with friends: Ignore them and find a sneaky way to accomplish your goal.

Mike Piazza

professional baseball player

"The only person you are destined to become is the person you
decide to be."
RALPH WALDO EMERSON

Mike Piazza was the 1,390th pick in the 1988 Major League Baseball
draft. To put that in perspective, the draft doesn't even go half that
many rounds anymore; there were only 20 rounds and 615
selections in the 2023 draft.

Piazza's selection was a favor to his father more than a decision
based on a belief in his major league prospects. Piazza's father,
Vince, was a longtime friend of the then-manager of the Los
Angeles Dodgers, Tommy Lasorda. Lasorda was even the godfather
of Mike's brother, Tommy. Vince asked Lasorda to draft Piazza,
who at the time was a first baseman for Miami-Dade Community
College, where he hit .364 with three home runs and 23 RBI in 29
games. Before that, he'd been relegated to the bench while a
freshman at the University of Miami.

Despite years of focusing all his energy and spare time on becoming
the best baseball player he could be, there were plenty of skeptics

about whether Piazza would ever make the big leagues—much less have an impact there.

Piazza proved the doubters wrong; after converting to catcher, he debuted in the majors on September 1, 1992, and went on to hit .308 with 427 home runs and 1,335 RBIs over the next 16 years. He won the Rookie of the Year award in 1993, was a 12-time All-Star and won a Silver Slugger award as the best-hitting catcher in the league 10 times.

And in 2016, he was inducted into the Baseball Hall of Fame.

Not bad for someone who had no future in the sport, huh?

Mike Piazza was born in Phoenix, Pennsylvania, on September 4, 1968. Vince had grown up with visions of playing major league ball, but at 16, he quit school to help support his family.

"As soon as Michael could walk, I put a wiffle ball bat in his hand," Vince said. He gave Piazza a pair of hand grippers at age 5 to strengthen his forearms, eventually adding weights and a sledgehammer to Piazza's training. Piazza would swing the 10- or 12-pound sledgehammer a couple hundred times a day. Vince set up a batting cage in their backyard, and rain, sleet or sunshine, Vince would throw batting practice to his son, sometimes throwing up to 300 balls a session. And, of course, Piazza played little league baseball.

Piazza seems to have enjoyed it. According to Vince, there "was never enough baseball that I could give him."

"All he wanted to do was play ball," Vince said. "He was an unusual kid at that age. He wouldn't socialize too much or go to dances or date too much. He'd come home from a baseball game and go in the cage."

Piazza occasionally served as batboy for Lasorda's Dodgers, and on those occasions, Lasorda and the team's hitting coach gave him hitting instructions. Piazza also got hitting tips from Ted Williams, one of the greatest hitters of all time.

All the training paid off: He set a record for home runs (10) in his little league. In his junior year of high school, he hit over .500 and 12 home runs, and in his senior year, he hit 11 homers, marking him as one of the best players in Pennsylvania.

Even so, major league scouts were skeptical about him; they liked his power but thought he was slow, cumbersome and would be a defensive liability. Then he went to the University of Miami and sat on the bench. Even his one good year at Miami-Dade didn't attract the raving scouting reports needed to be drafted by a major league team.

When he was drafted, Piazza was determined to prove the skeptics wrong. And he worked just as hard as a professional as he had in the backyard as a kid who dreamed of making it to the big leagues.

Lasorda suggested that Piazza switch to catcher, where his power and hitting ability would be an advantage at a position traditionally focused more on defensive ability. If Piazza could make himself an average defensive catcher, he could possibly have a future in the big leagues, Lasorda reckoned.

Piazza worked hard on his abilities behind the plate as he progressed through the minor leagues, spending hours a day at his craft. He hit well, and it was a quick rise to the majors: His first professional season was in 1989 with the Salem Dodgers in the lowest level of the minors. By 1992, he hit a combined .350 with 23 home runs in 472 at-bats in AA and AAA—the two highest levels of the minors. That September, Lasorda's big-league team called him up, and he only returned to the minors for two injury rehab assignments.

In his official rookie season in 1993, Piazza hit .318 with 35 home runs and 112 RBIs and made the All-Star team. He was just getting started. Piazza would go into the Hall of Fame as one of the best-hitting catchers ever. He has the highest OPS (on-base plus slugging percentage) of any catcher, .942, well ahead of second-place Joe Maurer at .889. Piazza's 390 home runs are also the most by a catcher all time.

Remember how Vince talked about Piazza's singular focus on baseball? He never lost that: "I see it today with him. He wakes up, goes to the park and after the game, he comes home, and then he wakes up and goes out to the park again," Vince said in 1999.

WHAT'S INSPIRING ABOUT MIKE PIAZZA'S STORY?

Mike never gave up on himself. He loved playing baseball, and when no professional scout believed he had a future in the game, he worked hard to improve. Not only did he prove to the scouts and others involved in professional baseball that he could play at the major league level, but he also excelled and turned himself into one of the best players ever. All through hard work and focused dedication.

WHAT CAN YOU TAKE FROM THE STORY?

Block out the naysayers. If you're dedicated and work hard for the career you want, you can achieve it. It probably won't be easy, and it may not always be fun. And you will fail, and then the doubters will make themselves heard. But if you continue to work hard and learn from failures, you can achieve your dreams.

Claude Monet

painter

"Without experiencing criticism and rejection in life, it would be impossible to grow or improve yourself."
MWANANDEKE KINDEMBO

Today, Claude Monet is known as a great artist and innovator of Impressionism, a style of painting that sought to capture the fleeting effects of light and atmosphere, often painted outdoors in natural light. The style is characterized by unblended colors and small, visible brushstrokes that present the impression of form.

But like so many other innovators, Monet had to earn his way to fame by suffering and persevering through skeptics.

Monet was born in Paris, France, on November 14, 1840. He was 5 when his family moved to the Normandy coast. There, he played near the sea and on the beaches in the constantly shifting weather. This environment shaped his vision of nature and led to his Impressionistic bent later in life.

Monet's father, Claude-Adolphe, managed the family's thriving grocery business, and he wanted young Claude to follow in his footsteps. But the son had other ideas.

At 10, Monet entered the Le Havre secondary school of the arts. He also began hanging around local artists and learning from them. By age 15, he was known for his charcoal caricatures, which he sold for 10-20 francs. Around this time, he met Eugene Boudin, one of the first landscape painters in France to paint outdoors. Boudin introduced Monet to the style, and it would be his signature for much of the next 60 years of his life.

When Monet was 16, his mother died; at 19 and 20, he visited Paris, where he would sit in The Louvre by a window and paint what he saw. He also became friends with fellow artists. To his father's disappointment, instead of enrolling in further formal education at École des Beaux-Arts, Monet frequented the areas where advanced artists hung out, learning from them, and worked at Académie Suisse, an informal art school in Paris.

His informal training was interrupted in 1861 and 1862 as Monet served two years of a seven-year commitment with the Algeria military. When Monet contracted typhoid, his aunt Marie-Jeanne, with whom he lived after his mother died, got him released from the military if he promised to complete an art course at a university. Monet was disillusioned with traditional art schools, though, so he enrolled with the academician Charles Gleyre, a Swiss artist. There, he and other students explored new approaches to art, including the effects of painting outdoors, with broken color and rapid brushstrokes—which would soon become known as Impressionism.

Although oil landscapes had been painted since at least the 16th century, they were usually produced in the studio and, therefore, weren't direct impressions of nature. They were from imagination or memory. Monet's paintings were on-the-spot, real landscapes painted with natural light.

But, as with most things new, the establishment was confused by Monet's work. Many major institutions dismissed his pieces. For example, in the spring of 1871, the Royal Academy rejected his work for its exhibition.

Although he seemingly had no one interested in his works, Monet continued to believe in himself and in the art he produced. And slowly but surely, others came around to his way of thinking. In 1872 or 1873 (there's some uncertainty about the exact year), he painted "Impression, Sunrise," one of his most famous pieces. It was included in the first Impressionist exhibition in 1874.

After his wife, Camille Doncieux, the model in many of his early paintings, died in 1879 of tuberculosis at just 32, Monet resolved never to be mired in poverty again. This personal struggle and determination fueled his creativity, leading him to paint some of the most celebrated pieces of the time. These paintings would eventually be featured in exhibitions and would earn him wealth and worldwide fame.

Throughout the 1880s, he had exhibitions at the Paris Salon and Galerie Durand-Ruel in Paris. Durand-Ruel had increasing success selling Monet's paintings, and by late 1890—when he was nearly 50—Monet was prosperous enough to buy the house he was renting in Giverny, France, and the surrounding buildings and land.

By 1912, he was earning 369,000 francs per year—compare that to the average annual income for a laborer in Paris: 1,000 francs.

Monet created more than 2,500 works of art in his lifetime. When he died from lung cancer on December 5, 1926, he had made his fortune and left a permanent mark on art and the wider world.

WHAT'S INSPIRING ABOUT CLAUDE MONET'S STORY?

Claude was ahead of his time. He was determined to be a great artist, so he learned all he could from those around him. But he wasn't content with following current and traditional trends, so he tried something new. When he first produced his Impressionist-style landscapes, nobody was interested in exhibiting them because they were unlike anything else, anything accepted. But still, Claude continued to paint and create—more than 2,500 works in all. Eventually, he became not just wealthy but famous as well. We still mention him when talking about the greatest artists of all time.

WHAT CAN YOU TAKE FROM THE STORY?

When someone tells you that you're doing it wrong because that's not the way it's always been done, proudly show them your new way of doing whatever it is you're doing. Don't be scared to try a new style or an innovative way of doing something. And don't let the naysayers who cling to tradition discourage you. It's not just original thinking that will change the world; you need to take original action, as well.

your free gifts

Want even more inspiration? To say thanks for your purchase, I'm offering four FREE bonuses:

- Two additional profiles for additional encouragement
- 366 inspirational quotes (a full leap-year's worth!) to put you in the right mind frame for confronting adversity
- A yearly printable planner eBook so that you can turn your inspiration into action

To get instant access, just go to:

https://schafer.aweb.page/Opt-in

If you want to stay inspired and take steps toward living your best life, be sure to grab these free resources.

chapter 6: overcoming disabilities and bullies

According to the World Health Organization (WHO), 16% of the world's population currently has a disability. That equals 1.3 billion people.

And yet, people with disabilities are often bullied, harassed and treated like second-class citizens. Maybe they need more support, but, as the three profiles in this chapter illustrate, they can accomplish great things—just like anyone else.

Even more, as you'll read in the stories of Temple Grandin, Nick Vujicic and Lizzie Velásquez, they can use the unique perspectives their disability gives them to reaffirm the value of every life, resilience and acceptance. Where others see a disadvantage, Grandlin, Vujicic and Velásquez came to see the disabilities they were born with as an advantage. Each of these three uses their disability as a starting point for inspiring others to better lives.

Let that be an inspirational message to you: No matter what you look like, what malformations or speech impediment or intellectual disability you have, you can still forge an incredible life for yourself. As Vujicic proves, you don't even need arms or legs to do so.

Temple Grandin

professor, author, animal behaviorist, speaker and autism self-advocate

"There are no constraints on the human mind, no walls around the human spirit, no barriers to our progress except those we ourselves erect."
RONALD REAGAN

When Temple Grandin was 3, doctors told her mother that Grandlin would likely need to be institutionalized for life because of her "brain damage." Grandin later told how she would pick the fuzz off a rug and eat it and dribble sand through her hands—"I remember getting hypnotized doing this," she said. "If I had been allowed to do that all day, I wouldn't be here now."

"Here" is a renowned advocate for people with autism, an accomplished professor of animal science at Colorado State University, and a sought-after consultant to the livestock industry. "Here" is having a Golden Globe-winning biopic made about her and being named one of Time magazine's 100 most influential people in 2010.

"Here" is possible because Anna Eustacia Purves (now Cutler) ignored those doctors' advice. Instead, she taught her daughter basic social and life skills. She insisted that Grandin learn manners; she didn't say "stop" or "don't," instead stating what the correct behavior was. She hired a speech pathologist and a nanny who spent hours with Grandin playing turn-taking games.

Grandin didn't start speaking until she was 3, but when she found her voice, she started using it to improve the lives of animals and autistic humans. That "brain damage"—later correctly diagnosed as autism—gave Grandin a unique view of the world that she used to benefit others.

Mary Temple Grandin was born into a wealthy family in Boston, Massachusetts, on August 29, 1947. As a child, she craved deep-pressure stimulation, but she felt overstimulated when someone hugged or held her. Despite her "brain damage," it was clear she had high intelligence. Her parents sent her to a series of private schools to nurture that.

One day while visiting her aunt's Arizona ranch, she noticed cattle were restricted in a squeeze chute—a narrow corridor that separates an animal from the rest of the herd—for inoculation. The cattle immediately calmed down when pressure from the chute was applied. She thought something like that chute might apply the deep pressure she needed while at the same time calming down her hypersensitivity.

Inspired, she created The Temple Grandin Hug Machine. The hug machine—also called the hug box, squeeze machine, or squeezebox—effectively placed her in a sort of squeeze chute between two sideboards hinged into a V shape that applies deep pressure to the body.

The machine broke through her tactile defensiveness, and she felt the love and concern of the people in her life and could express her feelings about herself and others.

"Many times in the squeeze chute I had pleasurable sensations and thought about love," she writes in *Emergence: labeled autistic*. "As a child, I had wished for a cubby hole about three feet wide and three feet high. The squeeze chute I ultimately built was that secret, coveted cubby hole of childhood dreams."

However, the boarding school psychologist disapproved of the device. "Well, Temple, I haven't decided whether this contraption of yours is a prototype of the womb or a casket," he said. The conversation got more condescending from there:

> "Neither," I said.

> He shifted his chair. Then, clearing his throat, he leaned across his desk as though sharing a secret. "*We* do not have an identity problem here, do *we*? I mean, *we* don't think we're a cow or something, do *we*?"

> "Are you crazy or something? Of course, I don't think I'm a cow or something. Do you think you're a cow?"

> "You've done some bizarre things here at Mountain Country School, Temple, and the staff has tried to have empathy and understanding. But this squeeze

box—it's weird. I have no choice but to advise your mother of my opinion."

The psychiatry department also thought the project was strange; it took the squeezebox away from Grandin and convinced her mother that the box was terrible for Grandin. But, in fact, their treatment and denial worsened her nerve attacks.

When Grandin was in college at Franklin Pierce College (now Franklin Pierce University) in New Hampshire, her old high school science teacher, Mr. Carlock, encouraged her to build a better box and do experiments with college students to examine why the squeeze box helped resolve anxiety and sensory issues.

That led her to perfect her chute into one that was gentle but with an amount of pressure that still couldn't be resisted. Her tests indicated a benefit with wider use: 62% of the 40 average college students who tried the machine liked it and found it relaxing. That justified her fixation with the chute. Further tests reinforced the feasibility of using the chute more widely.

Today, the squeezebox is a commonly used therapeutic tool for people with hyperactivity or autism.

Grandlin has said that she's an "object-visual thinker," meaning she processes information in pictures rather than words. To process information or solve a problem, she must "do the equivalent of a Google search" in her mind to access images. This unique perspective allows her to understand and empathize with animals in a way that few others can. So, she took what she learned from designing her human squeeze box to create improved squeeze chutes and restraint systems that revolutionized the livestock industry by reducing stress and improving animal well-being in processing facilities. This benefited the animals and the industry's efficiency.

Her empathy with animals has led her to be a well-respected voice in the livestock industry, a sphere that men dominate. After graduating with a bachelor's degree in psychology from Franklin Pierce College, she earned a master's degree from Arizona State and a doctorate in animal science from the University of Illinois.

When asked by Medscape if she thinks she would have achieved all that she has if she weren't autistic, Grandin says: "I don't think so, because there was a motivation that I had that a nonautistic person doesn't have. And I had a visualization skill that goes beyond what most people have. When I designed a piece of equipment, I could actually test-run it in my head like these virtual-reality computer programs. And I didn't even know that other people couldn't do this. That's the positive side of autism."

Grandin no longer needs the squeezebox; it broke in 2008, and she never fixed it. "I'm into hugging people now," she told Time magazine in 2010.

WHAT'S INSPIRING ABOUT TEMPLE GRANDIN'S STORY?

Temple didn't let her autism hold her back—instead, she used it as a springboard for innovative ideas that have changed therapy for others with autism and revolutionized the livestock industry.

WHAT CAN YOU TAKE FROM THE STORY?

Conditions will never be perfect. You may have a disability or just an inconvenience putting you at a disadvantage. Don't let it hold you back. Believe in yourself and lean into whatever is putting you at a disadvantage; maybe you transform it into an advantage. At the very least, understand that your disability doesn't have to hold you back. You can still live a great life and achieve the things you want to accomplish.

Nick Vujicic

motivational speaker, author and entrepreneur

"As a disabled man, let my life be a reflection of the endless amount of ability that exists within each and every one of us."
STEPHEN HAWKING

Nick Vujicic was born without arms or legs, but he's accomplished more in 40 years than most people with all their limbs accomplish in a lifetime. He's also perhaps the most hopeful, optimistic person you could ever meet.

Of course, he wasn't always this way. Vujicic was born on December 4, 1982, in Melbourne, Australia, with a rare congenital disorder called tetra-amelia syndrome. His parents were initially overwhelmed by his condition, and his mother refused to hold him as a newborn. But they quickly accepted his condition and taught him to be thankful for what he does have instead of bitter for what he lacks.

"If my parents never told me that I was beautiful the way I was, if my parents never told me that I was special and that I was loved, I wouldn't be here today," he said in his TedxNoviSad Talk titled "Overcoming Hopelessness."

Others mocked and bullied him when he was a child. They told him he would never get a job, get married, hold a woman's hand, or hug his children. "What kind of a father are you going to be if you can't even pick up your kids when they're crying?" they asked him. At age 8, he thought everyone would be better off if he were dead. He tried to drown himself in six inches of water when he was 10. "I had enough. I had enough. OK?" he said.

However, he realized that his suicide would be an added burden for his parents and brother. The only thing worse than caring for a child with no arms or legs is to have that child take their own life.

But he remained bitter and angry at the world and God. He would beg God for the miracle of his arms and legs appearing. But that, of course, would never happen. While reading the Bible one day when he was 15, he came across chapter 9 in the Gospel of John. In it, when Jesus sees a blind man, his disciples ask him whose sin had caused the man to be blind. "Who sinned, this man or his parents, that he was born blind?"

"Neither this man nor his parents sinned," Jesus replied, "but this happened so that the works of God might be displayed."

Jesus healed the man's sight, but the deeper message—that God made each of us to serve His purpose—resonated with Vujicic. It changed his perspective. He started to examine the purpose behind his disability. That's when he realized that, sure, he had physical limitations, but much of his suffering was because of his attitude and how he placed little value on himself. He accepted that he has value as a person—and that he has a purpose in life: to spread the message of hope and resilience.

He had finally internalized the messages his parents had been teaching him.

"In life, you have a choice: bitter or better? Choose better, forget bitter," he has said.

In that Ted Talk, Vujicic said: "We're all looking for something. We're all looking for hope. Hope you can't just have just because you were born with hope. No, we're born with pain. We're born and live through difficulties."

Vujicic still has his difficulties, but his attitude and how he approaches life aren't among them. By realizing his value, he has accomplished great things. He became the first special needs child to be integrated into the mainstream education system in Australia. He was awarded Young Citizen of the Year in 1990. He started giving inspirational speeches at schools and events. His message—and his sincere delivery—caught on, and he has become one of the most in-demand motivational speakers in the world. He's traveled to more than 75 countries and presented on more than 3,500 stages, talking to hundreds of millions of people.

He's also a multimillionaire, best-selling author and, yes, a husband and father of four. He has a nonprofit ministry, Life Without Limbs.

If Vujicic can reach this level of accomplishment, so can you.

"The human spirit can handle much worse than we realize. It matters how you are going to finish. Are you going to finish strong?" he has said.

Another motivational quote: "We easily become trapped in the 'someday' mentality. Someday, I'll have all the money I need to enjoy life. Someday, I'll be able to spend more time with my family. Someday, I'll have time to relax and do what I love doing.

"Today is the day!"

For more on Vujicic, check out his books and watch his Ted Talk: https://www.youtube.com/watch?v=6P2nPI6CTlc.

WHAT'S INSPIRING ABOUT NICK VUJICIC'S STORY?

Nick is trapped in a body without arms or legs. He could easily have given up on a meaningful life, and most people wouldn't have blamed him. But instead, he realized his value as a person and that he has purpose. His disability presented him with an opportunity to make a difference in the world by spreading a message of hope, resilience and a purposeful life.

WHAT CAN YOU TAKE FROM THE STORY?

"We may have absolutely no control over what happens to us, but we can control how we respond," Nick has said. Understand that your attitude will often determine your outcomes. Remember that you have value, and with the right attitude, you can accomplish great things and go far in life.

"If you can't get a miracle, become one," Nick also says.

Lizzie Velásquez

motivational speaker, author and activist

"Hard things are put in our way, not to stop us, but to call out our courage and strength."
UNKNOWN

"The World's Ugliest Woman."

That was the name of a YouTube video that Lizzie Velásquez came across when she was 17 years old. The video had more than 4 million views and thousands of comments.

The video was of her.

Elizabeth Ann "Lizzie" Velásquez was born on March 13, 1989, in Austin, Texas, with Marfanoid–progeroid–lipodystrophy syndrome, which prevents her from gaining weight, leaving her with a deflated, skin-and-bones look. She has no body fat and has never weighed more than 64 pounds, is blind in the right eye and has limited vision in her left eye. Only two other people have been diagnosed with the disorder.

Doctors told her first-time parents that she likely would never talk, walk, crawl, think or do anything by herself. Her parents took her home and raised her the best they could. They filled her life with love and acceptance. Velásquez was unaware she was different than other children until grade school.

"When I started kindergarten, I had absolutely no idea that I looked different. No clue," she said in her Ted Talk titled "How do you define yourself?"

She continues:

> I couldn't see that I looked different from other kids. I think of it kind of as a big slap of reality for a 5-year-old, because I went into school on the first day, decked out in Pocahontas gear. I was ready.
>
> I went in with my backpack that looked like a turtle shell because it was bigger than me, and I walked up to a little girl. I smiled at her, she looked up at me like I was a monster, like I was the scariest thing she had ever seen in her life.
>
> My first reaction was, she is really rude. I am a fun kid, and she is the one missing out. So, I'll just go over here and play with blocks or boys. I thought the day was going to get better and, unfortunately, it didn't. The day kind of got worse and worse, and a lot of people just wanted to have absolutely nothing to do with me, and I couldn't understand why. Why? What did I do? I didn't do anything to them. In my mind, I was still a really cool kid. So, I had to go home and ask my parents, what's wrong with me, what did I do, why don't they like me?

And they sat me down and they said, "Lizzie, the only thing that's different about you is that you are smaller than the other kids. You have this syndrome, but it's not going to define who you are." They said, go to school, pick your head up, smile, and continue to be yourself, and people will see that you're just like them.

And so that's what I did.

There was no way Velásquez could hide her appearance, and so she and her family didn't try to. Velásquez's father, Guadalupe, was a teacher who openly talked about the causes of her appearance in class. Velásquez became a cheerleader.

But, like any teenager, she was self-conscious about her looks. She thought she was ugly and disgusting. She wanted to scrub the syndrome off. "I would wish, and pray, and hope and do whatever I could [so] that I would wake up in the morning and I would be different, and I wouldn't have to deal with these struggles. It's what I wanted every single day—and every single day I was disappointed," she said in that Ted Talk.

Then, she found that video. In the comments, one poster encouraged her to "do the world a favor. Put a gun to your head and kill yourself."

She "cried my eyes out" and wanted to fight back.

But then, something clicked: She realized that she dictated how she reacted to this incident, that she could choose to make it a good thing. She decided to be grateful for what she had. "I can't see out of one eye, but I can see out of the other. I might get sick a lot, but I have really nice hair."

She wasn't going to let these people—people she doesn't know and likely never would—define her. She was going to let her accomplishments define her.

Velásquez worked her "butt off" to make herself more knowledgeable and build a good life for herself, one full of accomplishments, because that was the best way to get back at those anonymous commenters and bullies and others who teased her. And she used their negativity as motivation. "I'm going to use them as a ladder to climb up to my goals," she decided.

She set goals of being a motivational speaker, writing a book, graduating college, and having a career and a family. She graduated from Texas State University with a degree in communications and an English minor. She's published four books.

The motivational speaker bit? She taught herself how to do that by watching online videos and reading everything she could find on the topic.

Now, Velásquez is an in-demand motivational speaker. In her Ted Talk, her humor and shining spirit show. Take 13 minutes to watch it; you'll enjoy it. You can find it at https://www.ted.com/talks/lizzie_Velásquez_how_do_you_define _yourself.

She finishes her Ted Talk with this plea: "I used their negativity to light my fire to keep going. Use that, use that, use that negativity that you have in your life to make yourself better because I guarantee you, guarantee you, you will win."

WHAT'S INSPIRING ABOUT LIZZIE VELÁSQUEZ'S STORY?

Because of her syndrome, Lizzie was teased and bullied from the time she entered grade school. She could easily have grown bitter and withdrawn from life. Instead, she used the negativity from others who called her a "monster" as motivation to live her best life, and now she's accomplished all her academic and professional goals.

WHAT CAN YOU TAKE FROM THE STORY?

Don't let others define who you are or how you live your life. Instead, prove them wrong when they call you weak or unable to do something you want to do. Use their comments as motivation to keep you on task and fuel your success.

"You don't have to live up to anyone else's standards, you don't have to look like anyone else, you don't have to compare yourself to anyone else. You being you is enough, and you putting your positivity and good vibes out into the world, once you get to that point, absolutely everything will fall into place," she said.

---

chapter 7: overcoming hostile elements

Sometimes, the obstacles we face are outside forces—and perhaps even the extremes of Mother Nature.

The three profiles in this chapter feature people overcoming those extremes—of swimming in shark- and jellyfish-infested ocean waters and exploring around the South Pole. But in each tale, the person reached deep within themselves and fought back. For Sir Ernest Shackleton, fighting back meant saving his life—and those of his crew. For Gertrude Ederle and Diana Nyad, it wasn't a matter of life and death; instead, it was a matter of accomplishing something that had never been done before and proving—at least to themselves—that they could endure and realize their dreams.

In all three cases, we see the resilience and fortitude of the human spirit. We see that when confronted with extreme elements trying to keep us from accomplishing our goals, we can push on and still be successful. We just need to reach deep to find our reserves of willpower.

Here are three lives that shine as examples of how to do that.

Gertrude Ederle

competitive swimmer and Olympic champion

"Whatever you do, you need courage. Whatever course you decide upon, there is always someone to tell you that you are wrong. There are always difficulties arising that tempt you to believe your critics are right."
RALPH WALDO EMERSON

The first time Gertrude Ederle tried to swim the 21 miles of frigid, choppy water between England and continental Europe, she made it about 14 miles before her coach pulled her from the water. He felt she was struggling in the rough tides and was too nauseous to continue.

Ederle sobbed as Jabez Wolffe pulled her out of the water. It seemed her dream of completing the grueling trek was over.

But Ederle, 19, didn't accept that; she soon went back to training and developed a revolutionary two-piece suit, and a year later, she completed the journey—even beating the record time of the five men who had completed the trip before her by two hours.

Born in New York City on October 23, 1905, Ederle became an avid swimmer at an early age. At some point during her childhood, Ederle contracted measles, a deadly disease. Fortunately, she survived, but she suffered severe hearing loss as a result. This becomes more noteworthy later.

Ederle left school as a teenager to train as a competitive swimmer with the Women's Swimming Association. It worked: Between 1921 and 1925, she achieved 29 national and world amateur swimming records, including seven records she broke in a single day and the three medals her relay team won at the 1924 Olympic Games.

The following year, Ederle became a professional swimmer and started swimming longer distances. Her first significant professional effort was a 22-mile swim from Manhattan's Battery Park to New Jersey's Sandy Hook. She completed the swim in seven hours and 11 minutes—faster than the previous record, which a man set.

That's when she turned her attention to swimming across the English Channel. The rough, jellyfish-filled waters weren't the only opposition she'd have to overcome: As with just about every athletic endeavor of the day, she was told a woman couldn't achieve the feat. Women were considered physically inferior to men. Girls even got physical education classes less often than boys.

When Wolffe pulled Ederle out of the water, it seemed the doubters were correct. But Ederle was determined to prove them wrong. She hired a new trainer and returned to training. She believed her first attempt had failed because the loose, heavy, one-piece bathing suit she wore kept filling up with water as she swam. So, she cut a lighter one-piece suit into two so that it wouldn't fill with water. Then, she slathered herself in sheep grease as a defense against the cold and the stinging jellyfish.

When she entered the water near Cape Gris-Nez in France, the waves reached six feet high. The water was freezing and full of jellyfish and sharks. By rule, she could take breaks if she needed to and could even get food, including chicken, fruit and soup, from her trainer, T.W. Burgess, who sailed in a tugboat with her family nearby. He could put the food directly into her mouth, but the two couldn't touch or Ederle would be disqualified.

Nearby, reporters were on a tugboat broadcasting her progress. As it became apparent that she was going to finish the swim, people flocked to Dover, Kent, England, and a vast crowd was there to greet her when she arrived. She was exhausted and could barely stand. But she'd done it—and in record time, too: 14 hours and 31 minutes, a record that would stand until 1950.

One negative side effect of the swim: Completing her great mission caused her hearing impairment to become worse, and she became almost completely deaf.

When she returned to New York, Ederle was again greeted by a vast crowd, with admirers thronging the streets along a ticker-tape parade in her honor. Mayor Jimmy Walker congratulated her, and President Calvin Coolidge called her "America's Best Girl" and invited her to the White House. For several years after, Ederle was a sports star and popular sensation on par with Babe Ruth or Charles Lindbergh. She did a profitable tour on the Vaudeville circuit, a traveling entertainment before the days of television. She also appeared in a short film about her life.

In 1933, Ederle suffered a severe back injury that prevented her from competing. In retirement, she taught deaf children how to swim. She was inducted into the International Swimming Hall of Fame in 1965 and the Women's Sports Hall of Fame in 1980.

Ederle died on November 30, 2003, at age 98. On the Upper West Side of Manhattan, near where she grew up, stands The Gertrude Ederle Recreation Center.

WHAT'S INSPIRING ABOUT GERTRUDE EDERLE'S STORY?

Sharks. Stinging jellyfish. Six-foot waves. Exhaustion. Prevailing "wisdom" that women weren't physically able to swim the grueling 21 miles between England and France. Getting pulled out of the water by her trainer on her first attempt. Nothing stopped Gertrude from accomplishing her dream of becoming the first woman to swim across the English Channel. And she did it two hours faster than any man had previously done it!

'When somebody tells me I cannot do something, that's when I do it," she said.

WHAT CAN YOU TAKE FROM THE STORY?

After failing to complete the crossing the first time, Gertrude didn't give up. She examined what caused her failure and took steps to overcome those problems. She designed a new swimsuit and covered herself in grease. That probably wasn't pleasant, but she was willing to do what it took to complete her goal.

When you're met with obstacles, take a similar approach: Figure out how you're going to defeat them and try again. And again, if you must. Never give up.

Sir Ernest Shackleton

explorer

"Most of the important things in the world have been accomplished by people who have kept on trying when there seemed to be no hope at all."
DALE CARNEGIE

On August 1, 1914, Sir Ernest Shackleton and his crew of 27 set out from Norway onboard the 144-foot HMS Endurance sailing vessel on a mission to become the first people to cross the Antarctic continent. Two years later, they returned home—never having made the crossing but, surprisingly, all alive. In the intervening two years, they had endured unimaginable hardships and setbacks.

Shackleton was no stranger to exploring. He'd been born February 15, 1874, in Kilkea, Ireland. In 1901, he joined Robert Falcon Scott's Discovery expedition to the South Pole, but he was sent home early because of bad health in March 1903. Shackleton disagreed with this decision and vowed to pursue his own expeditions to rival Scott. Scott's group got within 480 miles of the Pole.

Shackleton made good on his promise to pursue his own expeditions: In 1907, after a stint as a journalist, he mounted the Nimrod expedition, which became the first successful attempt to scale Mount Erebus, an active volcano, and locate the approximate location of the magnetic South Pole. The group made it to within 97 miles of the Pole before ice prevented further progress.

The journey back was difficult, however, and when the group arrived at base camp in February 1909, they discovered that the Nimrod had set sail two days early. Shackleton and the others set fire to the camp to signal the ship, which turned back and retrieved them a few days later. During this time, the group was forced to cut back to half rations. Shackleton cut back even further, giving part of his rations to an ailing team member. This sort of self-sacrifice was a crucial part of what made Shackleton a great leader, and it would serve him and the 1914 expedition team members well.

When Shackleton returned to England, he was knighted and made a commander of the Royal Victorian Order. His fame grew, and he was in high demand as a public speaker. Then he decided on his next adventure: the Imperial Trans-Antarctic Expedition on December 5, 1914, with 28 men—including Shackleton and a stowaway who became the ship's steward—69 dogs and a tomcat.

Norwegian explorer Roald Amundsen had reached the South Pole in 1912; Shackleton focused on crossing the Antarctic from the Weddell Sea to the South Pole and then on to McMurdo Sound.

They never even reached the South Pole.

Instead, on January 18, 1915, the Endurance became trapped in ice off the Caird Coast within a day's sailing of their landing spot—

"frozen like an almond in the middle of a chocolate bar," according to crew member Thomas Orde-Lees. There was no way forward or back; instead, the ice floe drifted further from their destination, taking the ship along with it as the ice slowly crushed the boat.

"Our position on the morning of the 19th ... the weather was good, but it was impossible to advance. Overnight, the ice surrounded the ship, and clear sea could not be seen from the bridge," Shackleton wrote in his diary.

The crew—all but one handpicked by Shackleton—lived on the drifting boat for 10 months until it finally sank. Then, they lived on the ice floe for five months. They salvaged what provisions they could from the Endurance before it sank, but they were forced to abandon anything heavy or resource-depleting. This included books, tools, keepsakes and some of the younger dogs that were too small to pull their weight.

The men tried to march across the ice toward land, but they made just seven and a half miles in seven days, so they abandoned that plan. "There was no alternative but to camp once more on the floe and to possess our souls with what patience we could till conditions should appear more favorable for a renewal of the attempt to escape," Shackleton wrote in his diary.

The ice floe floated north toward Clarence and Elephant islands, then, on April 9, broke up. Shackleton ordered the men to climb into three 22.5-foot lifeboats. But now they were in the open ocean, with nothing solid supporting them except the bottom of the boats. Freezing spray rained down on them, and the ocean batted the boats from side to side. The men hunkered down into fetal positions as they dealt with the elements, seasickness and dysentery. They were unable to light fires for warmth or to melt ice for drinking water.

Finally, after six wet days, the exhausted, thirsty adventurers made it to Elephant Island. "At least half the party were insane," wrote Shackleton's second-in-command, Frank Wild. They were now 497 days into their expedition.

They were once more on solid ground, but they were stranded and unlikely to be rescued. The island was covered in snow and ice and beaten by strong winds. Shackleton knew they needed to leave quickly for South Georgia and its whaling fleet base. Doing so would require them to travel more than 800 miles on one of the most dangerous oceans in the world aboard the James Caird, one of those small lifeboats.

After reinforcing the boat's keel and soaking its fabric in oil and seal blood to make it waterproof, Shackleton and five others left Elephant Island on April 24, 1916. They had determined their route using a stopwatch and a sextant.

Shackleton stocked enough food for only four weeks. If they didn't reach their destination by then, they likely never would.

The six men navigated huge waves and 62-mile-an-hour winds. When they finally neared South Georgia after 15 days, they had to fight through a fierce storm to get to the island. But they made it.

Finally, the ordeal was over—but, no, it wasn't. The whaling stations were on the other side of the island; going back out into the ocean to sail around the island was a non-starter. So, they hiked across unexplored icy mountains. Shackleton drove nails into his shoes to turn them into crampons, a traction device attached to footwear to improve mobility on snow and ice during ice climbing. They covered the 18.5 miles to the Stromness base in just 36 hours. There, he organized a rescue effort for the men left behind on Elephant Island. Those men, meanwhile, survived by eating seal meat, penguins—and their dogs.

Even in organizing a rescue effort, though, there were obstacles. The United Kingdom was fighting in World War I and couldn't spare the resources. So Shackleton enlisted help from South America. On August 30—four months after he left—Shackleton returned to Elephant Island and brought the other 22 stranded adventurers aboard a Chilean ship.

It had been two years and 22 days since the group had set sail from England. All were returning. Shackleton's strength of will and leadership had pulled the men through the ordeal.

The next successful crossing of South Georgia was in 1955. The men who completed that crossing remarked how surprised they were that they'd managed the crossing, given their limited equipment and supplies—both of which were probably more copious than Shackleton and his team had. They may not have had the life-or-death motivation he had, though.

Shackleton swore off adventuring forever—but no, of course he didn't. In 1921, he set sail for Antarctica again. He was a celebrity, and a cheering crowd saw him off as he departed London. But in the port of Grytvyken, South Georgia, he died of a heart attack.

In 2022, 107 years after the Endurance sank, the Falklands Maritime Heritage Trust located its remains.

WHAT'S INSPIRING ABOUT SIR ERNEST SHACKLETON'S STORY?

After his ship wrecked in the Weddell Sea off Antarctica, Ernest and his team didn't have any choice but to fight the cold, wind and wetness to survive. Despite being stranded for more than 18 months, every person on Ernest's crew survived thanks to his outstanding leadership and grit. It shows what people are capable of when faced with adversity—far more than we think when sitting at home on the couch.

"I chose life over death for myself and my friends. ... I believe it is in our nature to explore, to reach out into the unknown. The only true failure would be not to explore at all," he said.

WHAT CAN YOU TAKE FROM THE STORY?

Realize that you can handle more than you think you can and that when faced with adversity, you may discover a well of strength and resilience you didn't realize you had. Continue to fight when faced with obstacles.

As Ernest said: "Difficulties are just things to overcome, after all."

Diana Nyad

long-distance swimmer, author, journalist and motivational speaker

"A hero is an ordinary individual who finds the strength to persevere and endure in spite of overwhelming obstacles."
CHRISTOPHER REEVE

At age 64, Diana Nyad became the first person to swim from Cuba to Florida without the protection of a shark cage. It was no easy feat: She finally succeeded on her fifth attempt over 35 years. But after each previous failure, she adjusted and came back again and again until she accomplished her goal.

Nyad was born in New York City on August 22, 1949, and was taught by an Olympian and Hall of Fame swimming coach as a teen. In high school, she won two state championships in the 100-yard backstroke and had dreams of swimming in the 1968 Olympics. Those dreams came crashing down in 1966 when endocarditis, a heart infection, kept her bedridden for three months. When she was back in the water, she'd lost enough speed that making the Olympic team was no longer realistic.

So Nyad shifted her focus to marathon swimming. As she'd been with sprint swimming pre-heart condition, Nyad was one of the best at marathon swimming. She set the world record in 1970 when she finished a 10-mile swim in Lake Ontario in four hours and 22 minutes. She also set the record in the 22-mile Bay of Naples race in 1974 when she finished in eight hours and 11 minutes.

The following year, Nyad swam around the island of Manhattan in seven hours and 57 minutes, bettering the previous record by 59 minutes.

Three years later, she tried for her biggest feat yet: becoming the first person to swim the 110 miles from Cuba to Florida. Well, actually, the second: In July 1978, Walter Poenisch had completed the swim from Havana, Cuba, to the Florida Keys at the age of 65. He never filed for official recognition for his feat, and, besides his crew, there were no outside observers to verify the swim, so it was never officially recognized. He swam in a shark cage as protection.

Nyad, 28, didn't know about Poenisch when she entered the water in Havana, Cuba on August 13, 1978. She made it 76 miles over 42 hours with the winds and currents pushing her off course. Then the following exchange took place, as relayed by Sports Illustrated:

> "Everything went wrong," head trainer Margie Carroll sobbed to her. "You swam for 42 hours, but the wind pushed us too far west, and I'm so sorry, Diana, but I'm telling you now that you're not going to make it."

> "But couldn't I keep going?" Nyad pleaded, shivering despite the 85-degree temperature of the Gulf Stream. Her words were barely intelligible; her tongue and lips were swollen from the salt water. "If I swam for 40 more hours, couldn't I make it then?"

"It can't be done, Diana," said Rich du Moulin, her co-navigator. "The wind is too strong against you, the waves are too high, and three of the four engines on the shark cage are dead. No swimmer could make it now, not even you." He spoke softly, as if to a child.

"But I can't quit. Isn't there some other place to swim for, some island maybe?"

"There is no other place, Diana. Key West is still the closest point, and it's 60 miles away."

Nyad abandoned her attempt that day—and for 33 years.

The next year she swam 102 miles from the island of North Bimini in the Bahamas to Juno Beach, Florida, without a shark cage.

Then she went on with her illustrious career outside of swimming. She wrote three books and articles for *The New York Times*, *Newsweek* and other publications. She co-founded BravaBody, which provides online exercise advice to women over 40. She also hosted the public radio program *The Savvy Traveler* from July 2001 until the show ended in 2004.

But then she got the itch again—the itch to try the Cuba-to-Florida swim again. By then, Austrian Susie Maroney had completed the swim in 1997. Like Poenisch, she had used a shark cage.

Nyad decided to scratch the itch when she was 62, and this time, do it without a cage. She made her second attempt to cross the stretch on August 8, 2011 but had to abandon that attempt after suffering an allergy attack in the water. Her third attempt ended early because of man-of-war stings after 67 miles. Tumultuous weather wrecked her fourth attempt in 2012.

Finally, in 2013, she completed the underwater trek. She didn't use the shark cage, but she had shark divers who operated an "electric shark shield" and used long poles to bop sharks on the nose if they got too close. She also used a customized silicone mask to protect her from venomous jellyfish.

After 53 grueling hours fighting currents, jellyfish and her own mental and physical limits, Nyad staggered ashore in Key West on September 2, 2013. At 64 years old, she had become the first person confirmed to swim the passage without a shark cage.

There is some controversy surrounding Nyad. Some of the statements she makes about her accomplishments in her 2015 memoir, *Find a Way*, have proven to be exaggerated or downright false. The 2023 biopic based on her life, "Nyad," carries some of those claims and exaggerations.

Some critics even question pace inconsistencies during her historic swim. The World Open Water Swimming Association Advisory Board denied ratification of the crossing because of a lack of independent observers, incomplete records, and other irregularities.

But the fact remains: at 64, Nyad accomplished a goal that she had set for herself 35 years earlier. Sharks, jellyfish, an asthma attack, cold water, big waves, life, career, age—she didn't let anything stop her from achieving a grueling dream. "If you want to touch the other shore badly enough, barring an impossible situation, you will. If your desire is diluted for any reason, you'll never make it," she said.

WHAT'S INSPIRING ABOUT DIANA NYAD'S STORY?

It took five attempts and 35 years, but Diana accomplished her goal of swimming the 110-mile passage from Cuba to Florida. After her initial failure, she realized in her 60s that she still had unfinished business. It took four more tries, but she didn't give up. Her lifelong quest embodies the human spirit at its finest: resilient, determined and forever young.

WHAT CAN YOU TAKE FROM THE STORY?

Sometimes, it takes time. Time to mature to be able to physically or mentally accomplish our goals. Time to prepare. Time to gather the resources and tools we need. But when you have a goal, don't give up on it if you fail initially. And never think, "I'm too old." "You're never too old to chase your dream," Diana has said.

Diana has also said, "Every human being on this planet has their pain and their heartache, and it's up to all of us to find our way back to the light."

chapter 8: overcoming "insurmountable obstacles"

By "insurmountable obstacles," I mean the type of common inborn challenges that traditionally stunt greater success in life. Poverty. Loss of parents. Abuse. The loss of a husband left Madam C.J. Walker a poor, single mother. That's not the usual narrative that starts a tale about a millionaire in the making.

How about a little girl who lost the use of her left leg and foot at age 6 becoming "The Fastest Woman on Earth?" Again, this is not the start you would expect for a success story.

But these are two women who didn't let the adverse situations they found themselves in define their future. Wilma Rudolph had family support in overcoming her paralysis. Walker had to build her own business empire. Both women became great successes.

From these women, we can learn that where you are now and what you're dealing with and facing in the future don't determine where you end up. *You* make your future.

Wilma Rudolph

Olympic champion sprinter and international track and field icon

"Challenges are what make life interesting.
Overcoming them is what makes life meaningful."
JOSHUA J. MARINE

"My doctors told me I would never walk again. My mother told me I would. I believed my mother," Wilma Rudolph said.

Her mom was right; not only did Rudolph walk again, but she also became the first American woman to win three gold medals in track and field at a single Olympic Games. She was even dubbed "The Fastest Woman on Earth" after her performance in the 1960 Olympics.

But first, Rudolph had to overcome a childhood of ailments.

She'd been born prematurely in St. Bethlehem, an unincorporated community just outside of Clarksville, Tennessee, on June 23, 1940, the 20th of 22 children her father sired. As a child, Rudolph was stricken with double pneumonia, scarlet fever and polio. The polio left her with a paralyzed left leg at age 6, requiring her to wear a leg brace.

"I spent most of my time trying to figure out how to get [the leg braces] off," she said. "But when you come from a large, wonderful family, there's always a way to achieve your goals."

Her siblings took turns each day removing the brace and massaging her injured leg. Her mother drove her 90 miles roundtrip to a hospital in Nashville for therapy. These treatments worked; she soon went from hopping around on one leg to walking in the brace at age 8 to getting the brace off at age 9. Then, there was no stopping the budding athlete.

Rudolph's mother discovered her playing basketball in the yard with her brothers when Rudolph was 11. "After that, it was basketball, basketball, basketball," her mother said.

Rudolph played on the girls' team at segregated Burt High School and became an all-state player, even setting the state record by scoring 49 points in a game.

Then something happened that changed Rudolph's athletic future: Tennessee State University's track coach, Ed Temple, asked the Burt High track coach to form a girls' track team so he could turn one of the Burt High girls' basketball team's forwards into a sprinter. That turned out to be Rudolph. She just had natural ability: "I don't know why I run so fast," she said. "I just run."

While still in high school, Rudolph attended Temple's daily college practices and even competed on the collegiate level. She was just 16 when she competed in the 200-meter dash at the 1956 Olympic

Games in Australia, where she won a bronze medal in the 4x100-meter relay.

Four years later, at the Olympic Games in Italy, she won three gold medals—in the 100-meter and 200-meter dash and the 4x100 relay. The performance cemented Rudolph as one of the greatest athletes of the 20th century. The next woman to win three gold medals in one Olympics, Florence Griffith Joyner, would do so 38 years later.

Suddenly, Rudolph was a celebrity. When the track and field team competed in Greece, England, Holland and Germany after the Olympics, crowds came to see Rudolph run. Mounted police had to restrict her admirers in Cologne. In Berlin, fans stole her shoes—and then surrounded her bus and beat on it with their fists until she waved.

Rudolph's performance gave her a platform, and she used it. Jackie Joyner-Kersee, who later won six Olympic medals, credited Rudolph for always supporting her. Joyner-Kersee's husband, Bob, said that Rudolph was the most significant influence for black women athletes.

In 1960, she used her influence for unprecedented societal change closer to home. When she returned from Rome, Tennessee Governor Buford Ellington planned to lead her welcome home celebration. But Ellington was an "old-fashioned segregationist," and Rudolph refused to attend the celebration if it was segregated. As a result, Rudolph's parade and banquet were the first integrated events in Clarksville. She would continue to take part in protests until segregation laws were eliminated.

Rudolph won the Associated Press' Female Athlete of the Year award in both 1960 and '61, and then she retired from track and field in 1962. She earned her degree from Tennessee State University and worked in education. Of course, she remained involved in sports: She worked at community centers throughout the United States, promoted running her entire life, was an assistant director for a youth foundation in Chicago to grow girls' track-and-field teams during the 1960s, and established the Wilma Rudolph Foundation to promote amateur athletics in the 1980s.

In 1974, Rudolph was inducted into the National Track & Field Hall of Fame; entry into the International Sports Hall of Fame followed in 1980, and the U.S. Olympic Hall of Fame included her in its first group of inductees in 1983. She also became the first woman to receive the National Collegiate Athletic Association's Silver Anniversary Award.

The indoor track and dormitory at Tennessee State University, as well as a street in Clarksville, are named in her honor.

Rudolph died of a brain tumor on November 12, 1994, leaving behind an impactful legacy that will live much longer than she did. And all because she refused to sit around when she was told she wouldn't be able to walk.

To learn more about Rudolph, check out her 1977 autobiography, *Wilma*.

WHAT'S INSPIRING ABOUT WILMA RUDOLPH'S STORY?

Wilma spent a lot of time in bed as a child. She contracted pneumonia, scarlet fever and polio, which left her paralyzed in her left leg and foot. But she underwent years of grueling physical therapy and treatments to regain her strength and mobility. Once she was able to walk unaided again, she discovered she had incredible athletic abilities, and she used them for everything they were worth. Then, as a celebrated athlete, she used her platform to advocate for civil rights and social change.

WHAT CAN YOU TAKE FROM THE STORY?

No matter what it looks like from your viewpoint, nobody's life is a piece of cake. Everyone struggles—and it's those struggles that make the victories sweeter. Remember that when the struggles get to be too much; think about how great it will feel when you accomplish your goals in spite of those pesky (physical or mental) obstacles.

"The triumph can't be had without the struggle," Wilma said.

Madam C.J. Walker

first self-made female millionaire in the United States

"Tough times are often fertile times for creativity."
KENNY WERNER

Madam C.J. Walker's "insurmountable obstacles" presented themselves early in life. Born Sarah Breedlove on a plantation in Delta, Louisiana, on December 23, 1867, to former slaves-turned-sharecroppers, she was orphaned at 7. She then lived with her older sister, Louvenia, and the two women worked the field for very little money. Meanwhile, at home, they suffered physical abuse from Louvenia's husband.

To escape that situation, Walker married Moses McWilliams when she was just 14—and then he, too, died just four years later, leaving Walker to care for their 2-year-old daughter, Lelia, alone. Walker moved to St. Lous, Missouri, to join her four brothers, who were barbers. There, she worked as a poorly paid laundress and cook for more than a decade.

Poverty seemed her natural, inescapable fact of life. But Walker refused to accept that.

During her time in St. Louis, she was mentored by teachers and members of the National Association of Colored Women. She also met Charles Walker, who would become her second husband and inspire the name of the company that she would turn into an empire on her way to becoming the first self-made female millionaire woman in the United States.

Walker suffered from a scalp disorder that caused her to lose much of her hair. She tried commercial hairdressings and experimented with her own formula to cure the disorder. Hers was a common ailment, like dandruff and other hygiene-related ailments, because the lack of indoor plumbing meant people washed their hair infrequently. She didn't like wearing hairdressings to cover her bald spots because she thought it would mark her lower social status—and she was trying to elevate herself.

Seeking a solution, Walker drew on her barber brothers' expertise in hair care to create some home remedies. This was when she developed the "Walker System," which involved scalp preparation, lotions and iron combs. She started using Annie Turnbo's Poro line of hair care products. These worked to some extent, and Walker became a Poro sales agent. That led her to Denver in 1905 with just $1.25 in her pocket; there she became a cook for a pharmacist who taught her the chemistry to perfect her pomade to heal scalps and spur hair growth.

The next year, Walker married Charles and began calling herself Madam C.J. Walker—a name she kept even after they divorced in 1910. Her breakthrough came in a dream, a divine intervention that led to the creation of a life-changing formula. "God answered my prayer, for one night I had a dream, and in that dream a big black man appeared to me and told me what to mix up for my hair. Some of the remedy was grown in Africa, but I sent for it, mixed it, put it on my scalp, and in a few weeks my hair was coming in faster than it had ever fallen out. I tried it on my friends; it helped them. I made up my mind I would begin to sell it," she said. This was the beginning of a journey that not only transformed her life but also had a profound impact on the lives of her customers.

The Madam C.J. Walker Manufacturing Company soon started selling Madam C.J. Walker's Wonderful Hair Grower, which included as its ingredients precipitated sulfur, copper sulfate, petrolatum, beeswax, coconut oil and a violet extract perfume to cover the sulfurous smell. The formula was similar to Turnbo's, and Turnbo advised customers to "beware of imitations." But really, the mixture of petrolatum and sulfur had been around for a hundred years, Walker's great-great-great-granddaughter and biographer, A'Lelia Bundles, noted.

Other early products from The Madam C.J. Walker Manufacturing Co. included a pressing oil and a vegetable shampoo. She encouraged customers to shampoo more often and follow the "Walker System."

To differentiate her products from others on the market, Walker emphasized her attention to the health of the women who would use the products. She sold her products to black women personally, an approach that won her loyal customers.

The company took off. In 1908, Walker opened the Lelia College of Beauty Culture and a factory in Pittsburgh, and in 1910, she moved the business's headquarters to Indianapolis because the access to railroads made it easier to distribute products. She traveled across the country hiring black women as licensed saleswomen, whom she called "Beauty Culturalists." These women would otherwise have been trapped in jobs as maids, cooks, laundresses and farmhands.

When she died in 1919 of hypertension, Walker employed about 40,000 people.

By that year, sales exceeded $500,000—about $10 million in today's currency. This turned Walker into a millionaire, and she was a wise real estate investor. Her New York mansion is a national historic landmark, as is the site of the Madame Walker Theatre Center; she purchased the property for the center, but it wasn't completed until 1927.

From sharecropping to a mansion—not bad for the daughter of slaves. Walker never forgot where she came from; as she became wealthy, she contributed to the YMCA, covered tuition for six black students at Tuskegee Institute, and became active in the anti-lynching movement. She bequeathed two-thirds of her future net profits to charity, along with leaving thousands of dollars to individuals and schools.

"I had little or no opportunity when I started out in life . . . I had to make my own living and my own opportunity," she later said, according to a biography written by her great-great-great-granddaughter. "But I made it. That is why I want to say to every Negro woman present, don't sit down and wait for the opportunities to come, but you have to get up and make them!"

WHAT'S INSPIRING ABOUT MADAM C.J. WALKER'S STORY?

Sarah Breedlove was born into poverty—and then things got worse. Her parents died, leaving her working and living with her sister and abusive brother-in-law. To escape that situation, she married at 14—then, shortly after the birth of their daughter, her husband died, leaving her poor and a single mother. But Sarah wouldn't give up; she was determined to make a name and fortune for herself, and she did that by creating haircare products that target black women and the problems of baldness and other hygiene-related issues they faced. Then, she worked hard selling her products and building a business. After branding herself Madam C.J. Walker, Sarah (aka Madam) became a millionaire.

WHAT CAN YOU TAKE FROM THE STORY?

Your current situation isn't your final situation. Nothing is inevitable. Work hard to accomplish your goals, never take no for an answer, and always look for ways to be innovative.

---

chapter 9: overcoming fear

This chapter has an odd mix of overcoming: fighting back against the Nazis and fighting back against the fear of a shark attack. Both seem farfetched. But these lives hold essential lessons for you.

Andree de Jongh was certainly fearful when she helped downed airmen escape capture by the Nazis. After all, she had to believe that capture almost certainly meant death. (Which, fortunately, didn't prove to be the case.) But she swallowed her fear and did what she could to help those men survive very real life-and-death situations. She did what was right, fear be damned.

Bethany Hamilton's fear maybe wasn't so urgent; the likelihood of being attacked by a shark once is one in 3.75 million. What are the odds of it happening again? But to Hamilton, the fear was understandably genuine. And it may well have weighed on her more than the fear weighed on de Jongh.

Both women, though, persevered through their fear and, as a result, lived or are living lives of consequence.

The lesson for you here: Don't let fear stop you. Fear is temporary. Your achievements are forever.

Andree de Jongh

World War II resistance hero

"When injustice becomes law, resistance becomes duty."
THOMAS JEFFERSON

When the Nazis invaded Belgium in 1940, Andree de Jongh quit her job as a commercial artist in Malmédy, Belgium, and moved to Brussels to work as a nurse. She had an ulterior motive: to help Allied airmen escape to freedom.

De Jongh was born on November 30, 1916, in Schaerbeek, Belgium, which at the time was occupied by Germany. After the end of World War I—right around the time de Jongh turned 2— Belgium regained its independence. But something had already seeped into de Jongh's consciousness; she grew up enamored with Edith Cavell, a British Red Cross nurse who had helped about 200 Allied soldiers escape to the neutral Netherlands during WWI. Cavell was executed in 1915, but she left a legacy that attracted de Jongh.

So, when WWII broke out, de Jongh couldn't just sit around; she wanted to follow in her idol's footsteps. Initially, nurse de Jongh helped captive prisoners in Brussels send letters home through the Red Cross. While doing this, she discovered that a number of British soldiers had escaped captivity during the German blitzkrieg and were hiding in safehouses throughout the area. As a nurse, de Jongh could freely move between the houses, relay messages and make connections between the houses. She also helped set up new safe houses and found trusted housekeepers to move them as needed.

But the safehouses were temporary and only slightly safe. De Jongh wanted to do more—she wanted to get the soldiers back to Britain. And do the same with any soldier who was shot down and not yet captured. So, in the spring of 1941, she partnered with Henri de Bliqui and Arnold Deppè to establish a route and resources to move escaped prisoners out of Belgium to neutral Spain—and then ideally on to Great Britain. The group called itself DDD because they all shared that letter in their names. Unfortunately, de Bliqui was arrested and executed after being betrayed by a Belgian collaborator in April 1941. That didn't dissuade de Jongh and Deppè; by June 1941, they had established a new route, the DD line. That 1,000-plus mile route from Belgium through France, across the Pyrenees into Spain and finally to the British territory of Gibraltar became known as the Comet Line.

The operation of getting these downed soldiers to freedom was complex. Organizers needed to recover the airmen who had been shot down before the Nazis did, get them civilian clothing and fake identity papers, deliver medical aid if needed, and shelter and feed the men as they moved along the line. It was so dangerous that de Jongh warned recruits they should expect to be dead or captured within six months. Her father, one of the organizers, was captured and executed with 22 others.

Yet de Jongh kept taking her charges along the route to safety. Between July 1941 and her capture in 1943, she led 24 to 33 expeditions to Gibraltar. Going by the code name Dédée—which means "little mother"—she escorted 118 servicemen to safety, and at least 300 more escaped along the Comet Line.

As de Jongh was escorting a soldier over the Pyrenees in January 1943, she was betrayed by a German collaborator and captured. During 20 interrogations, de Jongh took full responsibility for the operation, but the Germans refused to believe that someone as young as her (and, possibly, a female) could organize it. That saved her from execution; by the time the Nazi secret police realized she was telling the truth, they couldn't find her among the other prisoners at Ravensbrück concentration camp, from which she was released in 1945.

For her efforts during the war, the United States presented de Jongh with the Medal of Freedom with Golden Palm—the highest award to foreigners who helped the American effort during WWII. The citation said that de Jongh "chose one of the most perilous assignments of the war." Britian gave her its highest award for a civilian, the George Medal, and the French made her a Chevalier of the Légion d'honneur.

As for the Belgians: King Baudouin made her a Countess in 1985.

Certainly, Edith Cavell would have been proud. De Jongh resisted tyranny by putting her life on the line to save others, and in doing so, she didn't just preserve lives; she also showed that just because a pilot was shot down didn't mean they were lost. There was still a chance to save their lives.

De Jongh, who later worked in leper hospitals in the Belgian Congo and Ethiopia, died on October 3, 2007, at age 90.

WHAT'S INSPIRING ABOUT ANDREE DE JONGH'S STORY?

When war came to her country, Andree immediately decided to do something about it. She became a Red Cross nurse so that she could freely move between prisoners and help lead downed Allied soldiers and airmen to escape from Nazi-occupied Europe through an underground network known as the Comet Line. She did this at the risk of her own life—and was, in fact, captured. Her bravery resulted in more than 100 lives saved, while the Comet Line that she helped establish saved more than 300 soldiers and airmen.

WHAT CAN YOU TAKE FROM THE STORY?

If you see injustice and tyranny, stand up to it. It won't be easy, but it's the right thing to do. Always believe in something greater than yourself, even if doing so is risky or might make your life uncomfortable.

Bethany Hamilton

surfer and writer

"The brave man is not he who does not feel afraid,
but he who conquers that fear."
NELSON MANDELA

On Halloween morning in 2003, 13-year-old Bethany Hamilton went surfing with her best friend and her friend's father and brother at Tunnels Beach in Kauai County, Hawaii. In a lull between waves, Hamilton laid flat on her surfboard with her arms dangling in the water, chatting with the others.

Suddenly, her left arm was gripped from below and pulled by a powerful force. A 14-foot tiger shark had locked its teeth around Hamilton's arm and ripped it off just below the shoulder.

Hamilton managed to hold on to her board during the attack. The water turned red as her friend's family helped Hamilton back to shore. The father used a torn-up rash vest and leg rope for a tourniquet, and the family rushed Hamilton to Wilcox Memorial Hospital. When she arrived, Hamilton had lost more than 60% of her blood.

Coincidentally, Hamilton's father was at the hospital for scheduled knee surgery. He gave up his bed for his daughter and postponed his surgery.

Doctors saved Hamilton's life, and soon, she returned home and back to her normal life.

Surfing had always been a part of that normal life. Hamilton was born on February 8, 1990, in Kauai, Hawaii. By 13, she was competing in national surfing contests. But would surfing continue to be part of her everyday life after that encounter with a shark? Or would she let her justifiable fear keep her out of the water?

It doesn't seem as though Hamilton ever considered changing hobbies. Just a few weeks later, she was back in the water. Within months, she was surfing in competitions again.

"I guess getting back in the water was a little scary. I did have a little bit of a fear of sharks; I'd be lying if I said I didn't. However, I chose not to let it define me," she wrote on bethanyhamilton.com. "I could have been so scared of sharks, of being in the ocean and of surfing. I could have let my biggest fear of all—that I wouldn't be able to surf again—stop me in my tracks. However, I was willing to try, to put myself out there and to potentially fail."

In 2020, she told *The Guardian* newspaper: "[God] doesn't say that life's going to be easy peasy and perfect. … To think that we are not going to have trouble sets ourselves up for mental struggles, and the fact is we are all going to face hard times. When I lost my arm, I was just thankful to be alive, and that propelled me to have a more positive mindset."

Her parents, two brothers and the surfing community supported her in trying to get back into the water. Her father even fashioned a unique handle for her surfboard that helped her duck under oncoming waves.

At first, Hamilton would go out when the beach was crowded and stay close to the shore. She'd been out nearly half a mile when she was attacked, so closer to land felt safer. When she started going out further and surfing, she went to beaches where she was more comfortable as she slowly built up her confidence.

"I went from always looking underwater to nowadays I don't even think of sharks when I paddle out!" she wrote.

But Hamilton admits that it took her years to overcome that fear. She's managed to rationalize her fear, which has helped. "I decided to look at my fear from a factual perspective and realized that shark attacks are just sooo rare. I realized that I was way more likely to die from 1 million other things. It's literally more dangerous to drive to the beach or the grocery store in my car than it is to go out there to surf! That's when I decided that there was no reason to live my life in fear of such a rare occurrence."

Since then, Hamilton has built a career as a professional surfer in the free surfing arena. Since 2008, she has competed (and performed well) in the World Surf League, along with other special events. In 2017, she was inducted into the Surfer's Hall of Fame.

Hamilton is also a public speaker, using her experience to inspire others to overcome their challenges. The film "Bethany Hamilton: Unstoppable" tells her story. She has also authored or co-authored several books.

WHAT'S INSPIRING ABOUT BETHANY HAMILTON'S STORY?

So often, our fears are based on something imagined, something that only has power over us because we imagine it could be harmful. Bethany actually suffered the shark attack that caused her to fear returning to surfing. But she didn't let it keep her out of the water. She was determined not to let it define her. About a month later, she returned to surfing, and a year later, she was competing again. She didn't let her fear impact her life or what she wanted to do with it.

WHAT CAN YOU TAKE FROM THE STORY?

Don't let your fear define you or keep you from getting back in the water… or whatever you want to do. Plucking up courage can be difficult, but when you accomplish your dreams and goals in spite of your fears, you'll feel exhilarated.

"Feel the fear, and do it anyway," said Susan Jeffers, a psychologist and author of self-help books.

thank you

Before we conclude, I want to thank you so much for purchasing my book. I know you could have picked any of dozens of other books on this topic, but you took a chance and chose this one.

So, **thank you** for getting this book and for making it all the way to the end.

I hope you liked the book and now feel excited and ready to chase your dreams. Please do me a small favor: **Will you post a review on the platform? Posting a review is the best and easiest way to support the work of independent authors like me.**

Leaving a review will just take a minute. Simply scan the QR code below with your phone and you'll be taken to the Amazon page to review this book.

Your feedback will help me to keep writing the kind of books that inspire people to chase their dreams and live their best lives. It would also mean a lot to me to hear from you.

conclusion

Jadav Payeng

The Forest Man of India

"A seed grows with no sound, but a tree falls with huge noise.
From small beginnings come great things."
CHINESE PROVERB

When the floodwaters receded, they left behind hundreds of dead snakes.

For 16-year-old Jadav Payeng, the scene on the sandbar in the Brahmaputra River in 1979 marked a turning point in his life.

"The snakes died in the heat, without any tree cover," he later said. "I sat down and wept over their lifeless forms."

The sandbar filled with snake carcasses was (and still is) on Majuli, the world's largest river island, in the Indian state of Assam's Jorhat district. According to the 2011 census, the island has a population of more than 167,000. Over the previous century, the island had lost nearly 75% of its landmass. The river's flow had become so powerful that it eroded the strip that connected Majuli to the mainland, leaving that sandbar and washing away its trees and grass. The annual flooding caused by the melting of ice in the Himalayas became more severe, reaching new and dangerous levels.

Payeng stepped into this scene in 1979.

Jadav "Molai" Payeng was born October 31, 1959, in Jorhat, about a one-hour and 45-minute drive from Majuli.

After seeing the devastation from the flood and the dead snakes, Payeng realized that without trees, "…even we humans will have to die this way in the heat."

So Payeng decided to do something about it. He would restore life to the island.

Payeng had no experience as an arborist, so he asked the tribal elders about growing trees in the region. The men had seen the ravaging of the area repeatedly throughout the years and said that nothing could grow except bamboo. They gave him 20 bamboo seedlings, which he planted and nurtured with unwavering dedication. The seedlings were the only support he got from the elders or townspeople.

When the bamboo seedlings turned into a thicket, Payeng started planting other trees. Using a stick, he drilled deep holes into the land and poured seeds into the holes. He figured the trees' roots would bind the soil and soak up excess water, preventing future flooding.

"First with bamboo trees, then with cotton trees. I kept planting — all different kinds of trees," Payeng told National Public Radio (NPR) in 2017.

And, despite what the elders said, the trees survived—and thrived. Payeng has lost count of how many trees he's planted, but 45 years later, his "thicket" has turned into a 1,360-acre forest—larger, even, than Central Park in New York City. Christened Molai Forest, it's home to vultures, migratory birds, monkeys, tigers—including the endangered Royal Bengal tiger—and more than 100 elephants.

When residents, angered by elephants destroying their homes, wanted to cut down the forest, Payeng challenged them to kill him instead. The trees and animals were like his own children.

WHAT'S INSPIRING ABOUT JADAV PAYENG'S STORY?

Jadav saw a coming catastrophe and did something about it. He turned a dry, desolate land into a life-sustaining, lush, green forest. And it started by planting the seeds one day with faith that those seeds would grow into something more significant. They have, leaving us with an example of how a momentous transformation can begin with one small action.

WHAT CAN YOU TAKE FROM THE STORY?

Take action. Right now. No, really, when you put this book down, what can you do to plant the seed for future success? What small action can you take right now to hurdle the adversity and obstacles in your way?

We've seen 25 lives that attacked the adversity that stood between them and a successful, fulfilling life. That adversity came in many different shapes and sizes, and there are many more types not touched on in this book. But each profiled person overcame something and, in many cases, somethings in the quest to accomplish their goals. They're not extraordinary people. Or, at least, they weren't when they started. They made themselves extraordinary through their resilience, rejection of the status quo, and refusal to listen to the doubters.

You can be them. You can be extraordinary, no matter what you're facing today, tomorrow or the day after that. Those are just bumps in the road. You, you're tough, hardy and persistent. You just have to realize that. And I hope you throw a bunch of stubbornness in there, too.

Now, go change the world.

resources

Dr. Elizabeth Blackwell Biography | Hobart and William Smith Colleges. (n.d.). https://www.hws.edu/about/history/elizabeth-blackwell/biography.aspx

Elizabeth Blackwell | Biography & Facts. (2024, May 27). Encyclopedia Britannica. https://www.britannica.com/biography/Elizabeth-Blackwell

Woman Attends Medical School | Elizabeth Blackwell | History. (2003, May and June). https://www.hws.edu/about/history/elizabeth-blackwell/woman-attends-medical-school.aspx

Biography: Elizabeth Blackwell. (2015). Biography: Elizabeth Blackwell. https://www.womenshistory.org/education-resources/biographies/elizabeth-blackwell

How Elizabeth Blackwell became the first female doctor in the U.S. (2014, January 23). PBS NewsHour. https://www.pbs.org/newshour/health/elizabeth-blackwell-becomes-the-first-woman-doctor-in-the-united-states

Elizabeth Blackwell. (2021, March 31). *Biography.* https://www.biography.com/scientist/elizabeth-blackwell

Changing the Face of Medicine | ElizabethBlackwell. (n.d.). https://cfmedicine.nlm.nih.gov/physicians/biography_35.html

New York Infirmary for Indigent Women & Children – NYC LGBT Historic Sites Project. (n.d.).
https://www.nyclgbtsites.org/site/new-york-infirmary-for-indigent-women-children/

Elizabeth Blackwell: "That Girl There Is Doctor In Medicine" Part II. (2021, March 25). Circulating Now from the NLM Historical Collections.
https://circulatingnow.nlm.nih.gov/2021/03/25/elizabeth-blackwell-that-girl-there-is-doctor-in-medicine-part-ii/

Her Life - Frances Perkins Center. (n.d.). Frances Perkins Center.
https://francesperkinscenter.org/learn/her-life/

Settlement Houses. (n.d.).
http://www.encyclopedia.chicagohistory.org/pages/1135.html

Steinkopf-Frank, H. (2020, July 8). Frances Perkins: Architect of the New Deal. *JSTOR Daily.* https://daily.jstor.org/woman-architect-of-the-new-deal/

Corrigan, M. (2009, April 16). Frances Perkins, "The Woman Behind the New Deal." *NPR.*
https://www.npr.org/2009/04/16/102959041/frances-perkins-the-woman-behind-the-new-deal

Martin, R. (n.d.). *Red Scare | Definition, U.S. History, & Causes.* Encyclopedia Britannica.
https://www.britannica.com/topic/Red-Scare-politics

Women with Storie to Tell: Fanny Mendelssohn (1805-1847) (n.d.). Fiona Leonard.
https://www.fionaleonard.com/blog/2019/8/12/women-with-storie-to-tell-fanny-mendelssohn-1805-1847

Davis, E. (2018, November 21). *Fanny Mendelssohn: discover her biography, compositions and other facts.* Classic FM.

https://www.classicfm.com/composers/fanny-mendelssohn/fanny-mendelssohn-biography-compositions-facts/

Neill, C. (2023, June 30). *Fanny Mendelssohn: A Musical Prodigy and Forgotten Legacy*. History Hit. https://www.historyhit.com/culture/fanny-mendelssohn-a-musical-prodigy-and-forgotten-legacy/

Composer's Corner: The Story of Fanny Mendelssohn Hensel. (n.d.). Scales and Arpeggios. https://scalesandarpeggios.com/composers-corner-who-was-fanny-mendelssohn-hensel-and-why-is-she-still-important/

Hayman, S. (2017, March 8). A Fanny Mendelssohn masterpiece finally gets its due. *The Guardian*. https://www.theguardian.com/music/2017/mar/08/fanny-mendelssohn-easter-sonata-premiere-sheila-hayman

Guiberteau, O. (2023, August 29). *Bobbi Gibb: The Boston Marathon pioneer who raced a lie*. BBC Sport. https://www.bbc.com/sport/athletics/66615089

Ross, A. (2018, March 18). The Woman Who Crashed the Boston Marathon. *JSTOR Daily*. https://daily.jstor.org/the-woman-who-crashed-the-boston-marathon/

Harris, S. (2020, September 7). *The Story of Kathrine Switzer: The Running Legend Who Ran the Boston Marathon When Women Weren't Allowed*. My Modern Met. https://mymodernmet.com/kathrine-switzer-boston-marathon/

English, C. (2015, October 8). *"Not a Very Edifying Spectacle": The Controversial Women's 800-Meter Race in the 1928 Olympics*.

Sport in American History.
https://ussporthistory.com/2015/10/08/not-a-very-edifying-spectacle-the-controversial-womens-800-meter-race-in-the-1928-olympics/

Dupont, K.P. (2011, June 26). *Memoirs of marathon's first lady.*
Boston.com.
http://archive.boston.com/sports/marathon/articles/2011/06/26/memoirs_of_marathons_first_lady/

MARATHON'S ELITE WOMEN RUNNERS DEFY SPRING SNOW TO SPEAK AT WELLESLEY COLLEGE. (n.d.).
http://web.wellesley.edu/PublicAffairs/Releases/1996/041096.html

Gabarre, K. (2024, April 12) In 1967, She Broke Rules To Run the Boston Marathon—Today, She Says: 'Women Have Hidden Potential'. *The Healthy.*
https://www.thehealthy.com/exercise/kathrine-switzer-interview-every-womans-marathon-2024/

Stone, M., & D'Onfro, J. (2014, October 2). *The Inspiring Life Story Of Alibaba Founder Jack Ma, Now The Richest Man In China.*
Business Insider. https://www.businessinsider.com/the-inspiring-life-story-of-alibaba-founder-jack-ma-2014-10

MacLeod, C. (2014, September 17). Alibaba's Jack Ma: From 'crazy' to China's richest man. *USA Today.*
https://www.usatoday.com/story/tech/2014/09/17/alibaba-jack-ma-profile/15406641/

D'Onfro, J. (2014, May 7). *How Jack Ma Went From Being A Poor School Teacher To Turning Alibaba Into A $168 Billion Behemoth.*
Business Insider. https://www.businessinsider.com/jack-ma-founder-alibaba-2014-5

Jack Ma's 4 Failed Stories Tell Failure is the Mother of Success. (n.d).
Ecommerce Strategy China.

https://www.ecommercestrategychina.com/column/jack-mas-4-failed-stories-tell-failure-is-the-mother-of-success

Zitelmann, R. (2019, November 4). The Jack Ma Story: Why Thinking Big Is More Important Than Technical Knowledge. *Forbes.* https://www.forbes.com/sites/rainerzitelmann/2019/11/04/the-jack-ma-story-why-thinking-big-is-more-important-than-technical-knowledge/?sh=61a004f4419c

#49 | Jack Ma (n.d.). https://www.bloomberg.com/billionaires/profiles/jack-y-ma/

What is the advantage of cyclone vacuum cleaner? (n.d.). Maircle. https://maircle.com/blogs/blog/what-is-the-advantage-of-cyclone-vacuum-cleaner

Swallow, T. (2024, January 31). Lifetime of achievement: Sir James Dyson. *Sustainability Magazine.* https://sustainabilitymag.com/articles/lifetime-of-achievement-sir-james-dyson

James Dyson. (n.d.). Dyson United States. https://www.dyson.com/james-dyson

Dowling, S. (2013, March 13). *Frustration and failure fuel Dyson's success.* https://www.bbc.com/future/article/20130312-failure-is-the-best-medicine

Colonel Harland Sanders. (2020, April 24). *Biography.* https://www.biography.com/business-leaders/colonel-harland-sanders

Rathi, R. & Hawelia, A. (2023, December 22). *KFC Founder's Inspiring Journey: Colonel Sanders*. StartupTalky. https://startuptalky.com/colonel-sanders-kfc/

Gaspard, A. (2023, February 10). *A Look Into the Life of Colonel Harland Sanders*. A Touch of Business. https://atouchofbusiness.com/biographies/colonel-harland-sanders/

Pearce, J. E. (1982). *The Colonel*. Doubleday Books. http://books.google.ie/books?id=F9FnQgAACAAJ&dq=The+Colonel+:+the+captivating+biography+of+the+dynamic+founder+of+a+fast-food+empire&hl=&cd=1&source=gbs_api

Sanders, H. (1974). *Incredible Colonel*. http://books.google.ie/books?id=PQKtPAAACAAJ&dq=The+Incredible+Colonel&hl=&cd=1&source=gbs_api

Ozersky, J. (2012). *Colonel Sanders and the American Dream*. University of Texas Press. http://books.google.ie/books?id=dkVNCgAAQBAJ&printsec=frontcover&dq=Colonel+Sanders+and+the+American+Dream&hl=&cd=1&source=gbs_api

Darden, R., & Null, N. (2004). *Secret Recipe*. http://books.google.ie/books?id=h4vUAAAACAAJ&dq=Secret+Recipe:+Why+KFC+Is+Still+Cooking+After+50+Years&hl=&cd=1&source=gbs_api

NHIS - Teen. (n.d.). https://www.cdc.gov/nchs/nhis/teen.htm

Mental Illness. (n.d.). National Institute of Mental Health (NIMH). https://www.nimh.nih.gov/health/statistics/mental-illness

Sonnenberg, F. (2017, January 26). *A Remarkable Story About Overcoming Severe Anxiety*. Frank Sonnenberg Online.

https://www.franksonnenbergonline.com/blog/a-remarkable-story-about-overcoming-severe-anxiety/

Zimmerman, T. (n.y. September 16). *The Educator who Saved My Life.* Upstream Education. https://www.upstreamedu.org/bitesized-blog/the-educator-who-saved-my-life

Matthews, M. (2018, November 16). Kevin Love Explains What it Feels Like to Deal With Anxiety. *Men's Health.* https://www.menshealth.com/health/a25164905/nba-kevin-love-anxiety/

NBA Star Kevin Love Opens Up About His Struggle with Anxiety. (2023, May 19). Child Mind Institute. https://childmind.org/blog/nba-star-kevin-love-opens-up-about-his-struggle-with-anxiety/

Scipioni, J. (2021, November 18). *NBA star Kevin Love on finding success while struggling with mental health: "You can't achieve yourself out of depression."* CNBC. https://www.cnbc.com/2021/11/18/nba-star-kevin-love-on-mental-health-struggles-success-getting-covid.html

Love, K. (2020, September 17). To Anybody Going Through It. *The Players' Tribune.* https://www.theplayerstribune.com/articles/kevin-love-mental-health

Love, K. (2018, March 6). Everyone Is Going Through Something. *The Players' Tribune.* https://www.theplayerstribune.com/articles/kevin-love-everyone-is-going-through-something

Kevin Love on Trying to Achieve His Way Out of Depression. (2020, November 16). Harvard Business Review.

https://hbr.org/podcast/2020/11/kevin-love-on-trying-to-achieve-his-way-out-of-depression

Biography: Alice Coachman. (n.d.). National Women's History Museum. https://www.womenshistory.org/education-resources/biographies/alice-coachman

Antonucci, L. (2023, February 28). *Remembering History: Alice Coachman blazes pathway as first Black woman to win Olympic gold.* NBC Sports. https://www.nbcsports.com/on-her-turf/news/remembering-history-alice-coachman-blazes-pathway-as-first-black-woman-to-win-olympic-gold

Piccotti, T. (2024, January 24). George Washington Carver. *Biography.* https://www.biography.com/scientists/george-washington-carver

Carver, G. W. (ca. 1897). *George Washington Carver's own brief history of his life.* https://www.austintexas.gov/sites/default/files/files/Parks/Carver_Museum/Carver_Bio_and_Information.pdf

George Washington Carver | Biography, Education, Early Life, Inventions, & Facts. (2024, May 20). Encyclopedia Britannica. https://www.britannica.com/biography/George-Washington-Carver

George Washington Carver. (2023, January 5). The Linda Hall Library. https://www.lindahall.org/about/news/scientist-of-the-day/george-washington-carver/

Bro. George W. Carver (n.d.). https://www.pbswest.org/sigmatrailblazers/carver.html

16 Surprising Facts about George Washington Carver. (2023, June 2). https://nationalpeanutboard.org/news/16-surprising-facts-about-george-washington-carver/

On this day – *May 27, 1892 | White Mob Destroys Office of Ida B. Wells's Memphis Newspaper*. (n.d.). https://calendar.eji.org/racial-injustice/may/27

Tresniowski, A. (2021, March 5). *How Ida B. Wells Brought the Truth About Lynching to National Attention*. Literary Hub. https://lithub.com/how-ida-b-wells-brought-the-truth-about-lynching-to-national-attention/

Ida B. Wells. (2021, January 6). *Biography*. https://www.biography.com/authors-writers/ida-b-wells

Life Story: Ida B. Wells - Barnett. (n.d.) Women & the American Story. https://wams.nyhistory.org/modernizing-america/fighting-for-social-reform/ida-b-wells/

College Forum Volume 20 • Number 1 Page 20. (n.d.). https://www.bluetoad.com/publication/?m=12704&i=289779&p=20&pre=1&ver=html5

Berlind, W. (1999, October 18). Mike Piazza's 'Loudmouth' Dad Nervously Watches Mets Advance. *Observer*. https://observer.com/1999/10/mike-piazzas-loudmouth-dad-nervously-watches-mets-advance/

Holbrook, R. (n.d.). *The Life And Career Of Mike Piazza (Complete Story)*. Pro Baseball History. https://www.probaseballhistory.com/mike-piazza/

Mike Piazza Minor Leagues Statistics | Baseball-Reference.com. (n.d.). Baseball-Reference.com. https://www.baseball-reference.com/register/player.fcgi?id=piazza001mic

Seitz, W. C. (2024, June 1). *Claude Monet | Biography, Art, Water Lilies, Haystacks, Impression, Sunrise, & Facts*. Encyclopedia

Britannica. https://www.britannica.com/biography/Claude-Monet

Claude Monet Biography In Details (n.d.). Claude Monet The Complete Works. https://www.claudemonetgallery.org/biography.html

Eugène Boudin | Impressionist, Marine Painter, Normandy. (n.d.). Encyclopedia Britannica. https://www.britannica.com/biography/Eugene-Boudin

Selvin, C. (2020, November 13). *Monet's Magical Nuances: How the Impressionist Became a Worldwide Start.* ARTnews.com. https://www.artnews.com/feature/claude-monet-who-is-he-famous-works-1234576473/

Stańska, Z. (2024, May 21). *Claude Monet and Masterpieces Painted in Series.* DailyArt Magazine. https://www.dailyartmagazine.com/claude-monet-artist-painted-series/

Lewis, R. (2016, September 8). How Monet made his money: He was so obsessed with his work that he never stopped - even carrying on painting while the barber cut his hair. *Mail Online.* https://www.dailymail.co.uk/home/books/article-3780548/How-Monet-money-obsessed-work-never-stopped-carrying-painting-barber-cut-hair.html

13 Famous Paintings By Claude Monet. (2023, October 10). Singulart Magazine. https://www.singulart.com/en/blog/2023/10/24/claude-monet-paintings/

Disability. (2020, January 27). https://www.who.int/health-topics/disability#tab=tab_1

Autism First-Hand: An Expert Interview With Temple Grandin, PhD.
(n.d.). Medscape.
https://www.medscape.org/viewarticle/498153

Cutler, E. (2016). *A Thorn in My Pocket.* Future Horizons.
http://books.google.ie/books?id=b0wjMQAACAAJ&dq=
A+Thorn+in+My+Pocket&hl=&cd=1&source=gbs_api

Temple Grandin | Biography, Books, & Facts. (2024, May 30).
Encyclopedia Britannica.
https://www.britannica.com/biography/Temple-Grandin

Grandin, T. and Johnson, C. (2004, December 26). *'Animals in
translation.'* The New York Times.
https://www.nytimes.com/2004/12/26/books/chapters/a
nimals-in-translation.html

Grandin, T. (1986). *Emergence, Labeled Autistic.*
http://books.google.ie/books?id=13hHAAAAMAAJ&q=
Emergence+:+labeled+autistic&dq=Emergence+:+labeled
+autistic&hl=&cd=1&source=gbs_api

*Breaking News, Analysis, Politics, Blogs, News Photos, Video, Tech Reviews
- TIME.com.* (2010, February 4). TIME.com.
https://content.time.com/time/arts/article/0,8599,196034
7,00.html

The Nick Vujicic Story (n.d.). The STRIVE.
https://thestrive.co/nick-vujicic-story/

TEDx Talks. (2012, October 17). *Overcoming hopelessness | Nick
Vujicic | TEDxNoviSad* [Video]. YouTube.
https://www.youtube.com/watch?v=6P2nPI6CTlc

Velásquez, L. (2013, December). *How do you define yourself?* [Video].
TED Talks.

https://www.ted.com/talks/lizzie_velasquez_how_do_you_define_yourself

Livingstone, S. (2015, October 8). *A Brave Heart: How Lizzie Velásquez Battled the Bullies and Won*. Learning Liftoff. https://learningliftoff.com/students/inspiration-and-life-lessons/a-brave-heart-how-lizzie-velasquez-battled-the-bullies-and-won/

Gertrude Ederle 1926-1953. (n.d.). https://www.queenofthechannel.com/gertrude-ederle

Life Story: Gertrude Ederle, 1906–2003. (n.d.). Women & the American Story. https://wams.nyhistory.org/confidence-and-crises/jazz-age/gertrude-ederle/

Gertrude Ederle. (2021, April 6). *Biography*. https://www.biography.com/athletes/gertrude-ederle

Gertrude Ederle | Biography & Facts. (2024, June 1). Encyclopedia Britannica. https://www.britannica.com/biography/Gertrude-Ederle

Pettinger, T. (2018, Feb 28). *Sir Ernest Shackleton Biography*. Biography Online. https://www.biographyonline.net/adventurers/ernest-shackleton.html

South Pole exploration: Robert Falcon Scott, 1901–04. (n.d.). Royal Museums Greenwich. https://www.rmg.co.uk/stories/topics/south-pole-exploration-robert-falcon-scott-1901-04

Ernest Shackleton. (2022, March 30). *Biography*. https://www.biography.com/history-culture/ernest-shackleton

Mulvaney, K. (2024, May 2). *The Stunning Survival Story of Ernest Shackleton and His Endurance Crew.* HISTORY. https://www.history.com/news/shackleton-endurance-survival

The life of Ernest Henry Shackleton, the greatest Seafaring Adventure of all Time. (2020, September 8). Sail Universe. https://sailuniverse.com/2020/09/08/life-ernest-henry-shackleton-greatest-seafaring-adventure-time/

McEvoy, C., & Donica, A. (2023, November 3). Diana Nyad's Most Controversial Swim Inspired the New Netflix Movie Nyad. *Biography.* https://www.biography.com/movies-tv/a45523511/diana-nyad-movie-true-story

Florida High School Athletic Association. (n.d.). https://fhsaa.com/documents/2023/11/2/Swimming_Diving_Girls_2022_2023.pdf

Gum, L. (2016, November 4). *Lost at Sea: Walter Poenisch, his Cuba-to-Florida swim, and his stolen honor.* 614NOW. https://614now.com/2016/culture/community/lost-at-sea-walter-poenisch-his-cuba-to-florida-swim-and-his-stolen-honor

Levin, D. (n.d.). An Ill Wind That Blew No Good. *Sports Illustrated Vault | SI.com.* https://vault.si.com/vault/1978/08/28/an-ill-wind-that-blew-no-good-diana-nyad-failed-to-swim-from-cuba-to-key-west-when-adverse-winds-whipping-up-huge-swells-forced-her-out-of-the-water

Maass, H. (2015, January 8). *Diana Nyad's historic Cuba-to-Florida swim: A timeline.* theweek. https://theweek.com/articles/460490/diana-nyads-historic-cubatoflorida-swim-timeline

Hetherman, M. (2023, November 20). *The Real Clever & Complicated Life Of Diana Nyad -*. GO Magazine - The Cultural Roadmap for City Girls Everywhere. https://gomag.com/article/the-real-clever-complicated-life-of-diana-nyad/

Park, A. (2023, November 3). The Deeper Story Behind Netflix's *Nyad*. *TIME*. https://time.com/6330894/nyad-movie-true-story-netflix/

Wilma Rudolph. (2024, April 10). *Biography*. https://www.biography.com/athletes/wilma-rudolph

Roberts, M.B. (n.d.). *Rudolph ran and world went wild*. ESPN.com. https://www.espn.com/sportscentury/features/00016444.html

Engel, K. L. (n.d.). *Wilma Rudolph, Olympic gold medalist & civil rights pioneer*. Amazing Women In History. https://amazingwomeninhistory.com/wilma-rudolph-olympic-gold-medalist-civil-right-pioneer/

Michals, D. (n.d.). *Madam C.J. Walker*. National Women's History Museum. https://www.womenshistory.org/education-resources/biographies/madam-cj-walker

Bundles, A. (2024, May 20). *Madam C.J. Walker*. Britannica Money. https://www.britannica.com/money/Madam-C-J-Walker

How Madam C.J. Walker Invented Her Hair Care Products. (2021, January 19). *Biography*. https://www.biography.com/inventors/madam-cj-walker-invent-hair-care-products

Madam C. J. Walker - Products, Hair & Facts. (2024, February 20). *HISTORY*. https://www.history.com/topics/black-history/madame-c-j-walker

Madam CJ Walker: "An inspiration to us all." (2020, April 4). https://www.bbc.com/news/business-52130592

McLaughlin, K. (2023, December 5). *The chances of getting bitten by a shark while you're swimming at the beach are surprisingly low.* Business Insider. https://www.businessinsider.com/shark-attacks-what-are-odds-of-getting-bitten-2018-7

A 24-year-old Belgian woman created the largest escape line for downed airmen in WWII. (2023, May 18). We Are The Mighty. https://www.wearethemighty.com/history/andree-de-jongh-escape-line-for-downed-airmen-in-wwii/

Corbett, S. (2007, December 30). The Escape Artist. *The New York Times.* https://www.nytimes.com/2007/12/30/magazine/30dejongh-t.html

Martin, D. (2007, October 18). Andrée de Jongh, 90, legend of Belgian resistance, dies. *The New York Times.* https://www.nytimes.com/2007/10/18/world/europe/18jongh.html

Harmon, D. (2023, April 14). *Bethany Hamilton: A Story of Surfing, Adversity & Inspiration.* Surf Hungry. https://surfhungry.com/bethany-hamilton-a-story-of-surfing-adversity-inspiration/

Hamilton, B. (2022, August 23). *Getting Back on the Board: Overcoming Fear.* Bethany Hamilton. https://bethanyhamilton.com/getting-back-on-the-board-overcoming-fear/

Russell, G. (2020, March 6). Bethany Hamilton: 'My fear of losing surfing was greater than my fear of sharks.' *The Guardian.*

https://www.theguardian.com/sport/2020/mar/07/bethany-hamilton-unstoppable-film-my-fear-of-losing-surfing-was-greater-than-my-fear-of-sharks

Hahn, J. (2022, October 17). Surfer Bethany Hamilton Hopes to Show Kids How to 'Work Through' Their Fears in New Book. *Peoplemag.* https://people.com/sports/bethany-hamilton-book-interview-surfing-past-fear/

068. Jadav Payeng: The Forest Man of India (2020, July 26). INSPIRING STORY. https://inspiringstory.org/2020/07/26/jadav-payeng-the-forest-man-of-india/

Dimuro, G. (2018, November 22). *Meet Jadav Payeng: The "Forest Man of India" Who Created An Entire Forest Himself Over 40 Years.* All That's Interesting. https://allthatsinteresting.com/jadav-payeng

Majuli (District, Assam, India) - Population Statistics, Charts, Map and Location. (n.d.). https://citypopulation.de/en/india/admin/assam/760__majuli/

30-year journey from tribal boy to Forest Man. (2014, August 3). *The Times of India.* https://timesofindia.indiatimes.com/home/environment/developmental-issues/30-year-journey-from-tribal-boy-to-Forest-Man/articleshow/39510215.cms

McCarthy, J. (2017, December 26). A Lifetime Of Planting Trees On A Remote River Island: Meet India's Forest Man. *NPR.* https://www.npr.org/sections/parallels/2017/12/26/572421590/hed-take-his-own-life-before-killing-a-tree-meet-india-s-forest-man

About the Forest | Jadav "Molai" Payeng. (n.d.). https://blogs.ntu.edu.sg/hp3203-2018-01/enter-the-molai-forest/

Made in United States
Orlando, FL
12 December 2024

55465903R00095